Arlene Plevin writes rhapsodically about the joys of
cycling, in the manner of William Saroyan
that is as refreshing as the wind in your face on a
summer afternoon. She is also a veteran
cyclist of countless miles who gives us the practical
benefits of her experiences to make this
book well-rounded.
——Peter Nye, author of
Hearts of Lions and *The Cyclist's Sourcebook*

Bicycling has its share of how-to and where-to books,
but this one gives a little bit more—it never
forgets the essential why-to. Plevin's style is warm,
friendly, and inviting, and the solid
practical information here makes that invitation easy
to say yes to.
——Greg Cliburn, Senior Editor,
Outside magazine

HIKING
by Cindy Ross
RUNNING
by John Schubert
SAILING
by Michael B. McPhee

Forthcoming

CLIMBING

CROSS-COUNTRY SKIING

SCUBA DIVING

SKIING

CYCLING

A CELEBRATION OF THE SPORT AND THE WORLD'S BEST PLACES TO ENJOY IT

by ARLENE PLEVIN

Illustrations by David Taylor

Travel section by Joe Kita

A RICHARD BALLANTINE / BYRON PREISS BOOK

Arlene Plevin has explored Australia, Belize, Ireland, Canada, Baja, and most of the United States by bicycle. She received an M.F.A. in poetry from the Iowa Writer's Workshop in Iowa City, Iowa, where she participated in five RAGBRAIs (*The Des Moines Register*'s Annual Great Bicycle Ride Across Iowa). Plevin has been the Director of Publications at the League of American Wheelmen. Her work includes *The Bicyclist's Sourcebook* (co-authored with Michael Leccese) and articles in *Bicycling, Bicycle Guide, Southwest Cycling,* and *Caribbean Travel and Life.* She lives in Washington, D.C., where she commutes to work and play by bicycle.

Cycling: A Celebration of the Sport and the World's Best Places to Enjoy It

Series Editor: Richard Ballantine
Design Director: Byron Preiss
Editor: Babette Lefrak
Associate Editor: Brendan Healey
Contributor: Peter Oliver
Designers: Stephen Brenninkmeyer and Jennifer Winston
Illustrator: David Taylor
Cover Design: Fabrizio La Rocca
Cover Photograph: Marc Solomon/The Image Bank
Cover Illustrator: Marco Marinucci

Special thanks to Kristina Peterson, Publisher of Fodor's; Michael Spring, Editorial Director of Fodor's; Nin Chi, Kathy Huck, Nellie Kurtzman, Rosana Ragusa, Jessica Steinberg. Grateful acknowledgment is made for permission to reprint a portion of The Palm at the End of the Mind *by Wallace Stevens. Copyright © 1971 by Holly Stevens, reprinted by permission of Alfred A. Knopf, Inc., and to Story Songs Ltd. for permission to reprint a portion of Harry Chapin's song "Greyhound." Copyright © 1972 Story Songs Ltd.*

Special Sales
Fodor's Travel Publications are available at special discounts for bulk purchases (100 copies or more) for sales promotions or premiums. Special editions, including personalized covers, excerpts of existing guides, and corporate imprints, can be created in large quantities for special needs. For more information write to Special Marketing, Fodor's Travel Publications, 201 East 50th Street, New York, 10022. Inquiries from Canada should be sent to Random House of Canada, Ltd., Marketing Department, 1265 Aerowood Drive, Mississauga, Ontario L4W 1B9. Inquiries from the United Kingdom should be sent to Fodor's Travel Publications, 20 Vauxhall Bridge Road, London, England, SWIV 2SA.

MANUFACTURED IN THE UNITED STATES OF AMERICA.
10 9 8 7 6 5 4 3 2 1

*For Dr. Seuss and all my partners in crime
who shared their love of words and wheels with me,
especially my mother and father.*

CONTENTS

23 GREAT BICYCLE TOURS

INTRODUCTION

Not the early sun, not the water, the grace of late light,
nor the departure of dawn, but the wind I create from
my own movement, my world turning round.
                                                    —Laura Davids

I'm five or so miles west of Ellicott City, Maryland. Oak
leaves, bent back and golden, fall prematurely, swirling
around my wheels. The smooth road and mowed fields
fan out in all directions. Sunlight highlights what's left of
sprawling gardens, turning the tomatoes into brilliantly
red bits of punctuation.

LEMOND scrawled in three-foot-high letters slides
away under my wheel. Here in the hinterlands of Maryland, on the route for the 1991 Tour Du Pont cycle
race, some kids chalked their choice of champion in a
horrendous shade of lime green. Just three months ago,
locals thronged this country road. They made a day of
it—dusting off their old bicycles, maybe even oiling the
chains. Lauritzen, Hampsten, Grewal, Breukink, Phinney, Alcala, Bauer, and others whipped by. Grace and
elegance all wrapped in seemingly effortless motion.
One quick whirl of their wheels and they were gone—a
dream of movement.

For long moments, I pretend I'm in the peloton
behind the stars. I step up my cadence, stretch out over
the handlebars, and imagine my speed increases phenomenally. Momentarily, I am Davis Phinney, sprinting with
all my guts and making the bicycle surge. When I look

1

down, my odometer registers a very unimpressive twenty-three mph up this slight grade. So much for this reverie. But there are all kinds of victories, and all kinds of cyclists. There's any number of ways to catch the dream and make it real.

If I close my eyes for a second, images float up: mountain bikes, recumbents, tricycles, and racing bikes. Also unicycles, altered tandems, oddball contraptions with pontoons and pedals, and other quirky, fantastical inventions. A man I met, determinedly pedaling from Southern California to Washington's border and farther, also rises into view. Such strength of purpose, such pain. He had multiple sclerosis, and fatigue haunted him. We shared a root-beer float south of Zuma Beach, California. He loved his bicycle; his other set of legs, he called it.

There are my friends, several whom I've encouraged to set off on short rides. One, who rode for the first time on isolated, quiet roads, marveled at how different from city stop-and-go traffic bicycling in the country was. There's even my mother, proudly pedaling around her neighborhood and a bit beyond. Wearing the helmet and padded gloves I cajoled her into trying.

All of these people are the core of cycling. A sport, a way of being, with a lot of heart. It's hard to imagine that there was a time when I didn't bicycle. Difficult to consider a day not punctuated, shaped, and enriched by a commute to the post office for stamps or a quick spin around the park just to get my legs moving.

Certainly, I can't imagine myself without the heritage of distance touring, the long days on the saddle, the horizon opening before me.

Then there's the fun—water bottle ambushes, the quick flight back to kid behavior, great laughs with friends—the swoop of sudden speed and appreciation when hills are conquered. Retire to bicycling full-time and find a universe of earthly pleasures, a feast for the senses, populated by some of the most interesting people you'll ever encounter.

I'm biased. I do another kind of accounting, sometimes in miles (which I multiply by calories eaten) and sometimes in animals spied in the fields or the unexpected angle of shadows. I've found afternoon light—golden like a field of grain in the Loire Valley, or as if filtered through stained-glass windows—adorning the road.

Find the time, make the space for bicycling and for your capacity for awe. In one of America's favorite books, Huck Finn took to the Mississippi, fussed over encroaching civilization, the stiffness of shirts and buttons, opting instead to drift with the current.

While a raft adventure on the Mississippi was Huck's rite of passage, many choose bicycling as their sprint away from daily life. Thousands take to the road and look for themselves in America and elsewhere. The long ride, the cross-country tour, has become a ritual, a life passage.

I am happy not to know where my life begins and cycling ends. Simplicity and surcease. Instant philosophy and a great way to build calf muscles, spin stress into forward motion and memories. Let the bicycle be your confidant, doctor, friend, and buddy. Introduce others to it; put the romance of the road under everyone's wheels. There are more routes than any one person in his or her lifetime can tackle. The wonderful thing about bicycling is that there's always a way, and it's just outside your door.

A bicycle suits our purposes so closely; we get a bit more speed, but not enough to numb us. We pass among others, friendly and open. So here's to wherever the road or trail may bring you and whatever you may bring it. Whatever you want, envision it. The bicycle will help.

—*Arlene Plevin*

CYCLING

BEGINNINGS

The greatest poverty is not to live in a physical world.
　　　　　　　　　—Wallace Stevens, *The Palm*
　　　　　　　　　at the End of the Mind

I can start this a million different ways. Me. A bicycle.
Add a pillowcase stuffed with just-washed laundry
and a flat, ten-block pedal back from a laundromat on
Davenport Street in Iowa City. I've strategically balanced
the fat bag over one handlebar while compensating and
leaning slightly to the left. There's poetry and comedy in
this balance, plus a bit of fun.

I'm chuckling over how I must look. Mid-Iowa summer, unwieldy bag, my T-shirt riding up, my shorts and
socks inching down. Compounding this balancing act is a
six-pound watermelon precariously strapped to my bicycle's rear rack. Yes, I'm going to make the most of this
trip. I'm thinking, however, that I'd better not fall.

Daylilies bloom bright yellow across the street. On the
sidewalk, three kids on bikes with low-slung banana seats
slink by. They're wearing baseball hats backward. As they
pass me pedaling slowly in the street, they stand up, strut
a tad, and show off their bike-handling skills. It's a lazy
summer day, perfect for circling the block or riding to the
local swimming hole.

I've got all I can contend with portaging clean clothes
and watermelon. This is nothing new. As an impoverished student, my 10-speed is my transportation. It's these

two wheels or nothing.

And I don't mind. Among other things, bicycling challenges my ingenuity. I no longer feel as if I'm making do. I go to the food co-op, to work, and to classes by bicycle. I'm content arriving under my own steam and simply locking the bike to a pole, then sprinting off to class. Everything feels simple: whatever I need to carry or to do must be done on a bicycle.

This is how I began again as a cyclist. Sure, I learned as a kid. First the shiny red tricycle, then my patient parents, who ran alongside me as I awkwardly mastered the upright bicycle, moving from training wheels to just two wheels. I didn't think of bicycling as an athletic or sports activity. Nor did I make a commitment to bicycling for life. I just did it. Sports meant organized sports, and I had complete inability at any of that stuff. Team captains would come and go, picking taller, more coordinated folks for newcombe, softball, and so on. One by one, kids who could throw a ball, kick hard and far, or consistently connect a bat with a ball were chosen. I was more of an asset in girls' field hockey, but judging by the games my buddies and I played, you couldn't possibly consider field hockey an organized sport.

Back when I was a kid, fathers assembled bikes for birthdays or the holidays. The neighborhood was littered with bicycles of all descriptions. They leaned against fences, or were dropped wherever the owner felt like it. We didn't consider dings or dents or theft. We rode to the Good Humor man, planned brief journeys around the block, or rolled along on the boardwalk skirting the Atlantic Ocean. Our parents walked nearby, pushing younger siblings encased in strollers. Streamers hung in colorful abandon from our bikes' handlebars. Freedom and the means to go almost wherever was what the bicycle provided. However, like millions of Americans, the prospect of a driver's license seduced me, and as I got older, my trusty two-wheeled transport got relegated more and more to the garage. Somehow along the way I lost sight of cycling and grew away from those bicycle-induced discoveries, everything explored slow motion with all the senses treated to the sounds and smells of the road.

I began to reclaim the bicycle in college and graduate school. At first, it was because I was chronically impoverished. No car for me. I had this then-perverse pleasure in getting around entirely by bicycle. Did I need rice? Hop onto the bicycle down to Blooming Prairie Food Co-op. Would I meet a friend for a lazy cup of coffee and discussion in the Student Union's River Room? Sure, let me grab a lock and I'll be down in, say, the thirteen minutes it takes to glide there. I even cycled to a Halloween party dressed as a vampire. My long black cape flowed around me, shrouding the bicycle and looking, no doubt, like a coasting piece of cloth. With my preternaturally white face, blood red lips, and hooded cape, I must have given nightmares to at least one trick-or-treater.

When winter came (and it earns that name in Iowa), I tested my resolve and clothing supply. With the temperature hovering around zero, the wind whipping across the Iowa River, and streets glazed with snow, I'd go for long underwear, a mechanic's one-piece, zip-up

9

suit, two pairs of gloves, scarf, hat, two layers of socks, hiking boots, a hooded sweatshirt, and a Windbreaker. Feeling more pioneer than twenty-first-century person, I'd coast one hill and pedal heavily up two others to get the four miles to work. Ladling cooked powdered eggs and other delights to fellow students was my job. I often roasted in the dorm's cafeteria on those days; I had too much clothing on from my commute. This was pre-Gore-tex, pre-mass-distributed down feathers, hell, this was pre-extra pocket money days. On those winter days, I was a closet on wheels.

One contest I had with Art, another student, truly tested my doggedness. I bet at least two cups of hot cocoa that I could bicycle the deepest into the winter. My chin jutted out stubbornly as I said that. This I know. So come rain, snow, or shine, I gave the post office a run for its money. Except for one day.

I believe the thermometer rose to twenty degrees. The night before at least twenty inches of snow had been dumped on the area, on top of a previous layer of six inches. The roads weren't completely plowed. Cars slushed their way, somewhat diagonally, from one end of the city to another. I left my bicycle at home and decided to walk. Surely, I thought, Art wouldn't, couldn't be riding that day. As I plodded home from classes, I glanced right on Iowa Street. There, in the middle of the road, on his bicycle, mushed Art. He seemed blasé, as if surrounded by sunflowers, not snow. His 5-speed was more sled than wheels; nevertheless, he was riding it. My own stubborn self-reliance aside, he'd demonstrated remarkable stick-to-itness; he earned that hot cocoa.

As I renewed my interest in bicycling, I also discovered another part of me. It had been dormant, waiting to return. Just buried under pseudo-layers of adulthood and beginning responsibility. Up until that point, bicycling was somewhat eccentric, a fun way to get short distances. That all changed after one particularly stressful day of blood and guts. I can return to that day easily.

It's a typically hot and humid summer afternoon in Iowa City. Almost everyone is making some sort of inane comment like, "It's not the heat but the humidity." They talk about swimming pools, lakes, cold showers, and Alaska. While my summer job is in air-conditioned quarters, it is still particularly stressful. I'm a ward clerk in the operating room of the University of Iowa Hospitals and Clinics.

I've got a simple job here. I wear pale green scrubs and shoe covers, and, among other tasks, I post and update the operating room schedule, and get on the phone and the overhead speaker system in the event of a code blue. That translates into heart attack, get the head nurse and anesthesiologist to whatever operating room stat! And today, in a most unusual scenario, there have been two code blues. Everything has flowed smoothly, but I'm working on a major case of nerves. Stress is stacked on my chest like heavy boxes. I've seen one too many hurting people and the intensity of this well-paying summer job has finally gotten to me.

My shift is over. I toss my scrubs into a hamper, sighing. Someone said Governor Street out of town is a pretty road, and today is a good day to see if that's true. On with my baggy cotton shorts and equally loose T-shirt.

By the hospital's entrance, my first decent bicycle, a white mixte, is where I've locked it.

In moments the lock is in my canvas backpack, and I'm down the hill, past the university's gym, and across the swift Iowa River. Instead of pedaling home, I aim for Governor Street and then out Prairie du Chien Road. Well-kept rectangular homes line the road. With each stroke of the pedal, I am getting farther and farther from the hospital.

Suddenly the homes thin out. A long hill comes up under my heels, and down, down, down I go. Cooler air rushes past my face. Squat shrubs and other aspects of suburban landscape give way to a field thick with corn, a riverbed, and a fence amicably keeping cows from crossing a stream. The land fans open before me. I feel like Alice in Wonderland going through the mirror as I come up on the other side of the hill, pedaling strongly. Something catches in my throat.

The top of the hill yields a white farmhouse, set back from the road with a welcoming porch. There are pens with piglets frolicking like puppies. Corn rustles in the heavy June air, and my legs move smoothly, without thought. As the tenths of a mile turn into miles, my day of stress leaves me. I can almost see its ghost floating up into the sparse Iowa clouds. Crouched over my dropped handlebars, I notice grains of corn in the softening asphalt. An occasional cricket pings against my spokes. Small roads break off from the highway. I make a note to come back and explore them. A chestnut mare nickers to me. I whinny back, sounding no doubt like a rusty door hinge. In the distance, a tractor motors down a field. The

gently rolling hills have a kind of blue haze hovering over them: good ol' Iowa humidity at its best.

The road and all that I see and hear is mine. Just a few cars pass by. As I whirl along, watching and smelling everything, I think how wonderful this is. Behind a clump of black-eyed Susans, kittens tussle with their mother. Two dogs bark halfheartedly, barely lifting their heads from the shade of a large oak. Distance assumes another kind of relativity. I can see where I am going, and I have enough time to size up everything I approach.

The air smells green, moist with midsummer humidity. It's nourishing soybeans, corn, tomatoes, even pigs and cows. I am alone, but not lonely. The sounds of small farms, the animals feeding quietly, even the pungent smell of manure make up each minute. Second by second, I move farther from buildings, the daily pains, air conditioners, and other transitory things. This is a new world here. Somehow I know I will never be the same.

When I finally turn back, the Iowa sun is beginning to set. Losing its heat but leaving streaks of orange everywhere, it eases toward the horizon. The world is settling down: cows have been fed, the clatter of pigs nosing their buckets fills the air.

Maybe the quiet is an illusion. Maybe it just reminds me that all my noise—the tumult of my day—is left somewhere on the road. I, and I alone, can take my bicycle and go out into the country. Animals will not run away at my approach. I can leave behind aggravations and feel connected. And I have the means to do it. The very simple and accessible means. Beneath me is a beautifully elegant machine that, despite all sorts of manufacturers

Day Ride Pack

Here's where my very limited Girl Scout training and a bit of superstition shows up. I carry everything I think I might need, believing that I won't need it if I do have it and will desperately require it if I don't portage it. So on a typical day ride I carry the following. And no, it doesn't require a suitcase.

Extra food (snack stuff—food bar, dried fruit, etc.)
Rain jacket or Windbreaker
Swiss Army knife
Change
Pen and paper (I take notes at all times)
Map
Identification (includes necessary medical information)
Spare tube
Patch kit
Bicycle pump
Tire irons
Chain tool
Allen wrenches
Small sample of chain lube
Bandanna
Sunscreen
Lip balm

and designers, hasn't changed a heck of a lot since the early 1900s. Even I, with my simple and totally indifferent mechanical skills, can maintain it. And there is no glass shield between me and the world.

Becoming irrevocably seduced by cycling wasn't a long process. I'd already taken it for granted as quick and easy transport that just happened to be fun. That day in Iowa deepened my involvement with it. It also only hinted at the satisfaction bicycling could provide. I'd already enjoyed getting around in such an intimate, easy fashion. With progressively longer and longer rides, I found those two wheels took me back to childhood memories and were a quick conduit to feelings of independence and childlike joy. Yet I was more connected to my adult world. I moved at a human pace on the roads around me. I noticed things. I smelled honeysuckle, wild roses, and jasmine.

Initially cycling was a solitary affair. After work, during daylight-savings hours, I'd pedal off into the countryside. Gradually, I connected with the local bicycle shop, then other cyclists, and then the local bicycle club, enjoying the sharing of routes, great places to eat, and long rides.

The Bicyclists of Iowa City (BIC for short) loved rides out to the Amana Colonies and other places. Groups of ten or so of us would drift along tree-shaded routes or move a bit more quickly on treeless routes. On rides, both short and long conversations unfurled like flags. I talked about wind, infrequent flats, good places to cycle, and whether there was life after graduate school. Cycling proved to be a great way to forge friendships.

The miles to Kalona, Iowa, revealed prosperous, well-kept farms with somber Amish men standing on the floorboards of horse-drawn plows. Women in dark outfits with black bonnets would hang clothing up to dry while their children peered out at us. Gardens were lush. The community was small, apart from modern life and its distractions. While we never saw the Amish cycling, I believe the quiet way we traveled did not put them off. It is fitting that we, seeking solace and companionship, rode simply among the clapboard homes gleaming in the summer sun.

Cycling with clubs encouraged me to ride more and more, longer and longer. It also brought me to Marianne and Carol. The three of us were fairly close in age and somewhat similar in cycling ability. At the beginning, what I lacked in technique I made up for in stubbornness. Marianne, a nurse and printmaker, had a wry sense of humor. Carol came from a biking family; her husband liked to race. She kept up a wicked pace, even when she was in her sixth month of pregnancy and riding under a doctor's supervision.

While it was in the mid-seventies when few cyclists wore helmets, they knew better. Carol and Marianne wouldn't ride with me unless I bought one. And so I joined my first club, what I nicknamed the inverted soup-bowl contingent. Back then the only helmet was a Bell. The Bell Biker emerged in 1975 and has mercifully undergone numerous transmogrifications. Then sturdy, heavy, and irrevocably nerdy, those Bell brain buckets were the only helmet option around. And to my eyes, those clunky contraptions looked like soup bowls.

Soup bowls or not, the three of us often trudged out

and back on a five-mile stretch of Sand Road that hugged the Iowa River. I still can't understand it, but the wind was always, and I mean *always*, in our faces. I do recognize that one of the informal "maxims" of cycling was in operation—that whatever direction you ride in, the wind is against you. A cyclist's wind. Actually, meteorologists say that in most cases the wind can be counted on to subside or outright die around five P.M. Plan on that, however, and you'll end up with gale-force winds pelting you from all directions.

For us there were leisurely forty-mile pedals to West Liberty, a button of a town I renamed the village of big rolls. West Liberty had the Downtowner Restaurant, with a 300-pound chef who baked the most excellent cinnamon rolls. Inhale a lungful of sharp spices, fresh dough just sticky with glaze, and the fat molecules just laughed in delight. These rolls were the size of a dinner plate and cost a mere fifty cents. Perfect for carbohydrate loading.

It was after I'd eaten one and a half of those babies (a half more than usual), that I had my first fall as an adult. Actually, I can't blame the tumble on the cinnamon rolls; new cleats were the culprit.

I'm shifting to go up a gentle hill, and I overshift, the chain clunking over the freewheel and depositing in the spokes. Before I even have time to shift and get the sucker out—a trick that sometimes works—it jams, my cleated feet don't release me, and I fall over slowly, trying to get my right foot out and feeling like one of those characters on the old show "Laugh In." Of course the only thing hurt is my dignity and some skin on my

Wind

Bicyclists love wind . . . when it is behind them. Rare, this is. More often, the wind blows in your face.

Bicycling alone into the wind is, to put it bluntly, a drag. If at all possible, try and tackle gusty days with a friend or two. Then all of you can draft each other, taking turns at being in the front. When you do so, the front person takes the lead, the others tucking in behind him or her, following closely behind.

For drafting to work efficiently, your front wheel should be a foot or less away from the rear wheel of the bike in front, so you should all be skilled riders and take care to communicate information about the road's condition and if you are making any sudden moves, like stopping or braking. This way the front person not only breaks the wind for those behind but also supplies information crucial to safe cycling and drafting. The front rider pushes the hardest, but only for a short period of time.

Some bicyclists switch the lead every five minutes or every half mile. Racers will switch as frequently as every thirty strokes of the cranks. This way you take turns "fighting" the wind and it's not so wearying. With companions and a breakfront, the miles go quicker.

right kneecap. I catch myself with a padded glove (yet another reason to wear them).

From fat rolls in West Liberty, I moved on to RAG-BRAI, the *Des Moines Register's* Annual Great Bicycle Ride Across Iowa. This legendary cross-state ride was a natural for me. After all, like many students, all I'd seen of Iowa was the university and the local airport. A 500-or-so-mile ride from the western to eastern edge of Iowa would be one way to break in the saddle and me. RAG-BRAI was started by unsuspecting columnists Donald Kaul and John Karras in 1973 as a little cross-state ride with a few friends, but by the time I joined the ride in 1979, some 8,000 others had discovered it. So I was going to have a lot of company on my first big ride.

And I planned on rising to the challenge. As I put in long weekends, averaging seventy to eighty miles a day, my calves thickened. Even that recalcitrant muscle—ye ol' *gluteus maximus*—tightened up. I kept bicycling more and more—astonishing myself and others. I was no longer athletically inept. I felt like a lithe animal just eating up the miles. At this rate, I suspected I'd get a graduate degree on the strength of my quads, not my writing.

That first RAGBRAI showed me what was possible. Brueghel and Fellini couldn't have captured the panorama of cyclists and other oddities. People cycled in bathing suits, Day-Glo orange rain suits, and occasionally bona fide bike clothes. Tans of every variety were revealed in showers at local gyms (genders separated). Everyone was friendly. I survived my first hundred miles—my first century—in style, pulling in six hours and ten minutes after starting. I found folks from Sweden, California, and

Kansas. Team EATS (Everyone Always Takes Seconds) took me in, and I consumed more homemade ice cream in that one week than I had in a year.

RAGBRAI also whetted my appetite for longer rides, far from the maddening crowd. Not that RAGBRAI was jammed—I loved the variety: the groups of town kids who greeted you as you pedaled by, with a chorus of "Where ya from?" and "Give me five!" and the cyclist who courteously alerted others about his nasty habit, wearing a Warning: This Cyclist Chews Tobacco sign on his back.

I decided that seven days of just riding was too much fun to do once a year. Had to have more. Had to have days in the mountains, focused on weather, where to sleep, and food. So, I chose a three-week, 600-mile, self-supporting trip from Missoula, Montana, to Jasper, Alberta, Canada. I signed up with the non-profit organization, Bikecentennial, believing it would be good to have an expert leader along. I needn't have worried. Sure, tall Paul was helpful, a good guide, but if anything cemented my love of cycling more, it was miles of unbroken mountains, their royal presence. It was Logan Pass, four hours of uphill, and the sun setting on Glacier National Park, unsurpassed by anything I'd ever seen.

It was also the trip itself, uninterrupted by anything. Think of it: On most days, our world is thrust upon us, stacked with chores, must-dos, traffic, noise, and paperwork. Rarely are there opportunities for quiet, for just *being*. Maybe freedom can be defined as having all you need with you, simply eating when you're hungry, and having each day structured by appreciation. Look, a red-

23

tailed hawk circles that meadow like a halo. Purple lupine, devil's paintbrush, and daisies make a dandy place on which to take an afternoon siesta. Somehow it's easier to laugh, cry . . . well, hell, just be a part of the picture. Movement also helps sort out what's important. To know one's place in the scheme of things.

Pull with me into Jasper, Alberta, with 600 miles under your belt, and thirty or so odd pounds of dirty equipment on your 18-speed. Oreo crumbs, bits of melted socks (beware commercial dryers!), and a sense of accomplishment cling to the bicycle. Now see me leaning against my bicycle, its dirty panniers stuffed, the contents straining against the zippers. My unruly hair is fastened by a rubber band and my helmet rests on the sleeping bag and the rear rack. My calves and thighs are thick and competent, showing, no doubt, my peasant ancestry. Instead of working the fields, I'm out here pedaling the mountains. Pick me now, team captains, I think to myself.

I try to imagine some of those athletic despots from my childhood pedaling this distance. I can't. All I can see is the Canadian Rockies, the beautiful city of Jasper nestled in their hearts, and the thin trail of road leading out. This road travels far past any point I could have ever imagined. It threads into my future, now inseparable from my well-used black Trek bicycle.

Some of us start small. And I was definitely one of those. For me, bicycling began on a red tricycle, bright and shiny with a sturdy platform for passengers. If you were a buddy, you perched on the back, put your hands on my shoulders and rode with me up and down the sidewalk. That red platform with striations on it for extra grip was a way to woo friends. We rolled over cracks and hopscotch boards, studiously avoiding bugs. It's a good thing that concrete doesn't wear down easily, because I certainly would have worn a set of grooves in it if it did.

Amazing the ease with which I could pivot my tricycle. All of a sudden, the world extended its boundaries. I could cruise around the block with friends, my mother confident in my abilities. The natural limit of my range was my stamina—and how far my mother would let me go.

Learning how to balance a bicycle with training wheels was the next step. Despite my father's engineering skill with other equipment—gyros for NASA and such— I recall somewhat tippy training wheels. I went more side to side than forward, caroming around at uneven angles. Definitely not energy efficient.

Then there was a ritual of passage, making the miraculous leap from training wheels to balancing on two. Somehow, although I do it automatically now, I'm flabbergasted: two wheels and one and a half inches of rubber supporting a human body *and* going forward.

First solo on a bicycle—no training wheels, no support. I am seven and my parents are happy to help me bicycle "like a grown-up." I'm too big to have training wheels. So off they come, and here I go, courting chin plants, embarrassment, and other disasters.

My father trots alongside me as I bite my lower lip. This is a test. Can I move easily from lurching along on training wheels to gliding on two lonely wheels, free?

Can I do it without introducing my face to the ground? A fall seems unlikely; my father is all about me like a net.

"Put on some speed. That's it. Focus straight ahead. Don't look down." He adds, "It'll just take some practice." Now he encourages, "You can do it. Just keep pedaling."

I push the pedals stiffly, like I'm pushing steps. I'm conscious of everything: the need to balance, steer, lean a little forward, and most of all, pedal. I'm conscious of wanting my father to stay alongside me. His right hand is firmly in the center of my back. I can feel each fingertip individually, the thumb a bit more insistent. He's bending down and scooting along like a beetle. A bit out of shape, he breathes heavily.

"You're doin' fine." Already my eyes scan the sidewalk. I'm looking for obstacles and foolish people who haven't removed themselves from my lurching approach. I pedal harder, each stroke firmer. Neat frame houses with bright colors beckon. From the door of one, a friend pops out like a cork. She's going for a curbside seat for this lesson.

Somehow I move from teetering side to side to more of a straight line. Slowly, like a small plane taxiing down a runway, I move ahead of my father. His hand begins to leave my back; the fingers arch, bracing for one last gentle push. Then I take off. Orville and Wilbur Wright's first flight record of 120 feet, here I come. I spring forward, surprised at my new balance. A breeze lifts my sticky hair. The warmth of my father's palm stays in the center of my back.

I am going faster, then even faster past the maples. The force of gravity, as I understand it, anchors me to the planet *and* keeps me moored to training wheels, doesn't

snap me like a rubber band back to the saddle. I can stand up, pedaling furiously without crashing right or left.

I think I rode around the block again and again. I was awkward at dismounting and scared to stop. Was this balancing act a one-time miracle? Could I only master two wheels with my father starting me? I stopped, then started again. By myself. It's amazing what conquering a fear does for self-confidence.

Soon I could take my place in the street, or so I thought. My parents would have none of that, however, wisely knowing that street smarts would take a while. I was too young to understand that cars could permanently damage me and that looking right and left and right again wasn't enough. When I proved that I could obey traffic laws and ride predictably, they let me explore neighborhood routes.

Summer days would be spent cycling down the street to the Good Humor depot. Just around the corner, it was an unusually long room lined with cold silver freezers. More like a crypt than a place for crunchy chocolate éclairlike treats. On the sidewalk, a gang of neighborhood kids and I would straddle our bikes munching on ice cream and planning the afternoon.

The bicycle was a part of those long days of pure joy. We were outside, poking into everything. If we weren't at the beach, grinding sand into every towel, book, or fold of our bodies, then we were inventing stories sitting on our bikes or on swings under peach, plum, and crab apple trees. A burst of energy would compel us to swing a lazy leg over the saddle, and off we'd go.

Bicycling became a window for me. Imagination

dressed the road; different angles of approach revealed an entirely new neighborhood. The split-level homes on our street had all sorts of gardens and swing sets. Even pedaling in the yard, through the tall grass, was exotic. We called the latticed arbor, thick with purple grapes that the cardinals and chickadees loved, the Casbah. We believed there was something wicked and unusual about the word, having heard it whispered on some mysterious late-night television show.

Leaning on my handlebars, I'd survey the neighborhood. I could be Pocahantas scouting for John Smith. I was victorious; each roll of the wheel uncovered new land and helped Smith. Each time I straddled my bike, I packed a healthy dose of fantasy, and a sense of when I was supposed to be home. I was a pirate leaning at a rakish angle over the handlebars, I was the new around-the-block speed champion.

I decided to branch out from the short rides in the neighborhood. Envious, I studied older kids doing wheelies and cutting paths like half-moons on the sidewalk. They'd swing from side to side, their front wheel arching in a seemingly impossible way. Then, right before they'd go down in flames, they'd pull the wheel up, launching into the next half circle.

I wanted to do that. Defy gravity. Be cool. One Sunday I set out to mimic their grace and win admiration. With my parents fiddling somewhere on the lawn, I started small half circles on the sidewalk. Widening the arch more and more, I tested my agility. Whether I struck a deep dent between the sidewalk and the grass, I'll never know. Chin first, I hit the ground. Only it wasn't the ground, but unyielding and definitely unforgiving cement. The air knocked out of me, I struggled to cry. Strong hands eased me to a sitting position. I heard a rip. My father turned to face me, his face white. I could feel blood dripping down my neck.

My mother was there with a towel. By now, my father lagged behind, concerned but gagging. Through my haze, I realized he couldn't stomach blood and became useless at the sight of any one of his daughters' pain. Together we went to the hospital, leaving my blue bike sprawled in the grass like so much debris. I kept thinking, my teeth will fall out, and my parents will never let me bicycle again.

Numb, I determined the origin of that rip sound. As my father paced the hospital's hall, his red-and-white boxer shorts protruded from a huge gash in his pants. He'd split them from stem to stern and was completely oblivious to it.

I survived quite nicely, though my chin bore a ragged, crescent-shaped scar. Years later, I'd notice how most people seem to have landed chin first at some point in their life.

The memory of my first cycling injury faded quickly. So did other mishaps. Simple errors can become huge injustices when you are eleven. I stewed and stewed over a difference of opinion with my parents for a while. I can't even remember what it was, but I do remember, however, that I held it close and fed its mild poison before I decided to run away from home. Too young to drive and too pokey to walk, I chose my bicycle. A few coins were my supply; I didn't know where I was going.

Terra incognito, way beyond the known and my parents' domain, was my destination. Past the smaller children and their tricycles and scooters, past the Good Humor depot and its coolness, even across Long Beach Boulevard, the boundary of my world. I pedaled east, aiming like an arrow. Past homes that looked much like mine, on streets white in the midday glare.

I trembled with the newness of my scenery. Still my wheels led me on. Different people sat on porches, and an occassional mother pushed a stroller. No one looked up at me. I was just a kid on a bicycle.

My blue bike worked fine, wheels moving like a magic carpet. Everything was new. I felt like a conquistador, felt like naming everything I saw. I imagined the murmur of the end of the island, cupped my hand over one ear and heard the whisper of Montauk Point, Rockville, Massapequa, and other towns across the Long Beach bridge. I could get there by bike.

With each block I put between my home, I felt a tug. Would I run away entirely, leave my parents in another geography? On the small island I lived on, would I find a shack to make my own, be Friday to Robinson Crusoe, be Crusoe myself? With each spin of the wheel I dreamed.

Other streets bisected my main path. I was reluctant to take them and get lost. Like a stiff thread yanking me back, my thoughts kept returning to home. Perhaps an hour passed, perhaps two. Some of the anger dropped from my heart; it was, after all, due to a small, silly thing. I turned around to face west and the direction of my home. Would my parents be angry? Would they even

31

know I had been gone?

Finally, overwhelmed by uncertainty and a full bladder, I turned back. My home was where it should be. In the driveway, in the big blue boat of a 1964 Chevrolet, my father sat, examining a foldout map of Long Beach and Long Island. My mother was gathering my sister and the usual mess of diapers and bibs. "Where were you?" she asked, hugging me. "Put the bike away. We're going for a drive."

Maps, I thought. That's the secret. Maps took you elsewhere. Let you know where the earth ended and the oceans began. You could travel in any direction with a map. You could return to the very beginning of space. If, I thought, you could figure out how to fold them.

My father had, at this moment, handed the lumpy, creased mass to my mother, shrugging. With a smile she held the map, folding its sharp creases like a knife. A knife with which to open the world and spread it like cheese on your bread.

No one had even noticed my disappearance. My bike leaned against the garage, a riderless horse. It kept my secrets well.

RESOURCES
Teaching Someone to Bicycle

Whether you are helping an adult or a child learn to bicycle for the first time, there are several steps you can take to ensure it's a fun and successful experience. Whoever is learning should know that it will take some time and practice to feel comfortable.

It makes sense to find a calm spot, preferably one that's somewhat grassy and smooth. Interestingly, everyone I spoke with mentioned they'd been introduced to the fine art of balancing on two wheels at the top of a gentle incline. In that case, I guess gravity provides a gentle push if fear is prompting the prospective cyclist to be a bit reluctant.

First lower the seat of the bicycle so that the rider's feet can touch the ground. Show the person the brakes and how to use them, cautioning him or her to pump them instead of clenching them without letting up, and to apply the front brake sparingly. You may want to run alongside the cyclist, holding the saddle, while the person gets the hang of steering. Tell the person to look forward, not down, and to pedal firmly.

Bicycle builder and designer Gary Fisher started his son on a heavy-duty tricycle, first helping him turn the pedals. Later, he introduced him to a little bicycle with training wheels, put elbow pads on his knees, and found a soft lawn. Gary let go of the handlebars, but held the seat, letting his son steer. Gradually he let him glide and let go of the bike entirely. "He'd go for a while and then he'd fall down," Fisher laughed. Gary's son is still working on his new bicycle-handling skills. He's not too sure of the brakes or of putting his feet down, but then he's not yet four.

Author and bicycle expert Richard Ballantine creates a variation of the above. In addition to lowering the saddle, he takes off the pedals entirely, creating a sort of Draisienne—wheels, frame, and seat. He positions the cyclist-to-be at the top of a gentle incline, explains how to work the brakes, and then has them push along with their feet. The prospective cyclist quickly learns how to balance and steer, and as soon as they can coast for a good distance without touching a foot to the ground, the pedals are replaced and the cyclist is away. Ballantine claims the method is infallible, and takes fifteen minutes or less.

As anyone who has ever helped a friend knows, bring patience and humor to the classroom, wherever it may be. Meteorologist Bob Ryan recalls taking his seven-year-old son, new to bicycling, along the C & O Canal in Washington, D.C. His son took pleasure in racing fast and was merrily zipping along . . . until he hit an overhanging branch. Startled, he steered over the bank of the canal and into it. Bob remembers he was there one minute and then gone. Bob merely fished him out and they resumed cycling. Ah, the stuff of memories. □

Bike Clubs

Clubs are one of the great forces on the bicycle scene. Whether large or small, they provide a social hub for cyclists. Many offer a plethora of organized rides and events, while others have an advocacy bent and work to improve road conditions and educate trail users. People new to an area can quickly find out the best routes and enjoy the company of other cyclists on club rides. Beginning cyclists will find clubs a repository of all sorts of information on equipment and riding techniques. Here's a brief list of clubs. For information on local clubs, check out your nearby bicycle store, or contact Bikecentennial, P.O. Box 8308, Missoula, MT 59807, tel.: 406/721-1776, and League of American Wheelmen, 190 W. Ostend St., Ste. 120, Baltimore, MD 21230, tel.: 301/539-3399.

Another Dam Bike Club, c/o 1302 Robin St., Knoxville, IA 50138.

Baltimore Bicycle Club, P.O. Box 5906, Baltimore, MD 21208.

Bicyclists of Iowa City, P.O. Box 846, Iowa City, IA 52240.

Bike Psychos, P.O. Box 652, Oak Lawn, IL 60454.

Bloomington Bicycle Club, P.O. Box 463, Bloomington, IN 47402.

California Association of Bicycling Organizations (CABO), P.O. Box 2684, Dublin, CA 94568.

Cascade Bicycle Club, P.O. Box 31299, Seattle, WA 98103, tel.: 206/522-2453.

Charles River Wheelmen, 19 Chase Ave., West Newton, MA 02165.

Concerned Off-Road Bicycle Association (CORBA), 15236 Victory Blvd., Box 149, Van Nuys, CA 91411.

Denver Bicycle Touring Club, Box 9873, Denver, CO 80201.

Fat Apple, 244 E. 85th St., #1G, New York, NY 10028.

Florida Bicycle Association, c/o 210 Lake Hollingsworth, #1707, Lakeland, FL 33803.

Granite State Wheelmen, 16 Clinton St., Salem, NH 03079.

Greater Arizona Bicycling Association (GABA), Phoenix Chapter, P.O. Box 3132, Tempe, AZ 85281.

Grizzly Peak Cyclists, P.O. Box 9308, Berkeley, CA 94709.

Los Angeles Wheelmen, 2212 Charnwood Ave., Alhambra, CA 91803.

Louisville Wheelmen, P.O. Box 35541, Louisville, KY 40232.

Ohio Bicycle Federation, 9611 Lorain Ave., Cleveland, OH 44102.

Potomac Pedalers, P.O. Box 23601, L'Enfant Plaza Station, Washington, D.C. 20024, tel.: 202/363-8687.

SCOR Cardiac Cyclists Club, 12200 E. Washington Blvd., Ste. O, Whittier, CA 90606.

Washington Area Bicyclist Association (WABA), 1819 H. St. NW, Ste. 640, Washington, D.C. 20006, tel.: 202/872-9830. ☐

Rides

Any bike ride is worth doing. Some, however, are extra special—real memory makers—and have evolved over the years to include and encourage many cyclists. There are week-long excursions and one-day events. Many rides offer all sorts of help: sag wagon (support vehicle), water stops, rest areas, snacks, water bottles, maps, cue sheets, meals, and marked roads. At some point, consider joining up with any or all of the following. They already have a track record and promise to be around for a while longer.

Assault on Mt. Mitchell, Spartanburg Freewheelers, P.O. Box 6171, Spartanburg, SC 29304, tel.: 803/578-1181. Tough 100-mile century with a 32-mile, 5,000-foot climb up Mt. Mitchell. Start when it's early and cool and don't lollygag around the lunch stop.

Bicycle Ride Across Georgia (BRAG), c/o 887 Ryan Lane, Lilburn, GA 30247. Join 3,000 cyclists in mid-June for an eight-day, 350-mile, family-oriented ride across Georgia. Besides peaches, Georgia has some great savannah to see.

Bicycle Ride Across Tennessee (BRAT), Division of Parks and Recreation, Tennessee Department of Conservation, Nashville, TN 37243-0446. More than 500 cyclists participate in this seven-day, 470-mile ride in September. I've heard the scenery is spectacular.

Chequamegon Fat Tire Festival, P.O. Box 267, Cable, WI 54821, tel.: 715/739-6608. Two-day festival in September. This somewhat unpronounceable festival continues to attract such talent as Greg LeMond. Amazing to think it began in 1983 and attracted less than thirty cyclists. Now it's limited to 2,500, and riders get turned away.

Coast to Coast Bicycle Classic, Tim Kneeland and Associates, 200 Lake Washingon Blvd. Ste. 101, Seattle, WA 98122-6540, tel.: 800/433-0528, 206/322-4102. Cross-country, fundraising ride across United States. Offered once a year, beginning in Seattle in June and going 3,300 miles to Asbury Park, New Jersey. As many as 100 cyclists join up for this ride.

Conference Vélo Mondiale Pro Bike Vélo City, Vélo Quebec, 4575 boul. Saint Laurent, Bureau 310, Montreal, Quebec H2X 2T7, Canada, tel.: 517/847-8356 (September 13-17, 1992). International bicycle conference held every two years in a different country. A unique opportunity to meet and exchange ideas with bicycle advocates from all parts of the world. See you there.

Cycle Across Missouri Parks, AYH, 7187 Manchester Rd., St. Louis, MO 63143, tel.: 314/644-4660. A seven-day exploration of Missouri, in June. This can be a hilly ride, averaging sixty miles a day. Participants camp in state parks.

Cycle Oregon, tel.: 800/547-7842, 503/323-1270. A seven-day, 350-mile tour that varies each year. You can't go wrong in Oregon. Gorgeous scenery, swell folks.

Davis Double Century, Davis Bike Club, 610 3rd St., Davis, CA 95616. Here's your chance to do 200 miles the third weekend in May. This is a most famous ride, well known among the ultra-marathon cycling contingent.

GEAR, c/o L.A.W., 190 W. Ostend St., Ste. 120, Baltimore, MD 21230, tel.: 301/539-3399. Yearly June bicycle rally. Location varies. Attracts hundreds of league members from all over the country. Largest collection of old Bell Biker helmets.

Great Annual Peanut Rides, Emporia Bicycle Club, P.O. Box 631, Emporia, VA 23847. Send a self-addressed stamped envelope to this address and you'll receive information on one of my favorite rides. (I also happen to like peanuts.) There's a variety of flat rides, ranging from 13 to 100 miles. You'll find peanut sauce, peanut cookies, peanut candy, peanut sandwiches, and much more. This two-day is typically offered in early September, after the Labor Day weekend.

Hilly Hundred, CIBA, 5224 Grandview Dr., Indianapolis, IN 46208 tel.: 317/251-4130. In October, a favorite of mine. They've added a costume contest since I've participated. I understand a team costume won in 1991. The winners were on a tandem and single bike, dressed as Boo Boo, Yogi and Cindy Bear.

Human Powered Speed Championships, P.O. Box 51255, Indianapolis, IN 46251. Pedaling on water? Pontoons on land? Four-wheeled bikes? You can count on those and more at the American HPV Championships. Summer event, location varies.

Le Tour de L'Ile de Montreal. 3575, boul. Saint Laurent, Bureau 310, Montreal, Quebec, Canada, H2X 217, tel.: 514/847-8687. Largest one-day bicycle ride in the world. In 1991, more than 45,000 cyclists enjoyed the forty-mile (or less) ride that "transformed the island of Montreal into a vast bicycle path." First week of June.

London to Brighton, England. Bike Events, P.O. Box 75,

Bath, Avon, England. Another whopper, with 40,000-plus cyclists wending fifty-eight miles through the green lanes of Surrey to the seashore at Brighton. Masses of fuel stops and free "Doctor Bike" first aid. Early summer.

Midwest Tandem Rally, Tandem Club of America, c/o Jack and Susan Goertz, 220 Vanessa Dr., Birmingham AL 35242-4430. If you're not on a long bike, you're going to feel mighty uncomfortable here. Held in a different location each year, this rally features tandem lovers of all ages.

Moonlight Ramble, AYH, 7187 Manchester Rd., St. Louis, MO 63143, tel.: 314/644-4660. Riding at two A.M. with thousands of others can be romantic, even fun. Wheels whir quietly by the light of the moon. Police manage major intersections along the eight- and twenty-mile routes. The Moonlight Ramble brings out 19,000 cycling night owls for a ride through downtown St. Louis. The route varies each year and the ride traditionally happens the second weekend of August. Howling is optional.

Mount Dora Bicycle Festival, AYH, Florida Council, P.O. Box 533097, Orlando, FL 32853-3097, tel.: 407/649-8761. Famous three-day festival with something for everyone. Typically held in mid-October, it's generally full by the end of September. Goers to this event claim the food and friendly folks are not to be missed. Note that it's a fairly flat event, with a few hills thrown in for a view.

National Bike Ride, Anywhere, U.S.A., third weekend in May. Ride anywhere, any distance, celebration of bicycling. Receive a pin. Contact National Bike Ride Headquarters, P.O. Box 388, Bristol, VT 05443. Here's your chance to ride around the block or down the coast of California. Just participate in any fashion; take a friend on a bicycle ride and portage a picnic basket. Go out with your family to the local lake. It's a "just do it" kind of day.

Old Kentucky Home Tour, c/o 9004 Willowwood Way, Louisville, KY 40299, tel.: 502/491-7120. Two-day tour, typically in mid-September, attracting 500 cyclists. I can guarantee you'll see some green hills, graceful horses, and back-country roads. Nice way to spend a fall weekend.

RAGBRAI, *Register's* Annual Great Bicycle Ride Across Iowa, RAGBRAI, P.O. Box 622, Des Moines, IA 50303, tel.: 515/284-8282. Typically, it's the last full week in July, Sunday to Sunday, 500 or so miles. To even be part of the lottery for this event, send a self-addressed, stamped envelope by March 1. Bring your family and your appetite. Iowans know how to cook for thousands, and they love RAGBRAI.

Rosarito to Ensenada, Bicycling West, P.O. Box 15128, San Diego, CA 92175-0128, tel.: 619/583-3001. Join thousands twice a year on this legendary ride. Fine fish tacos.

Seattle to Portland, Cascade Bicycle Club, P.O. Box 31299, Seattle, WA 98103, tel.: 206/298-8222. Otherwise known as STP, this extraordinarily popular state-to-state ride attracts 10,000 cyclists who pedal 200 miles in one to two days. Rural, flat backroads and superb Northwest scenery distinguish this ride. Cyclists aren't stranded in Portland, however. They and their bicycles can take a bus back or, if the 200 miles hasn't been sufficient, bicycle back. Be sure to register early for this late-June ride. Registration opens in February.

TOARV (Tour of the Arkansas River Valley), Colorado Springs Cycling Club, P.O. Box 49602, Colorado Springs, CO 80949-9602. Third weekend in May for 185 miles.

TOSRV (Tour of the Scioto River Valley), P.O. Box 14384, Columbus, OH 43214, tel.: 614/447-1006. A 210-mile weekend ride that's more than thirty years old. Every year, whether it rains or beams, cyclists come out for this event. It's a classic in its field.

Tour Du Pont, Medalist, 1209 E. Cary St., Richmond, VA 23219, tel.: 804/354-9934. This ten-day bicycle race, held on the East Coast in May, provides great spectator opportunities. Get a seat on a curb or country lane and cheer your favorites. In 1992, the Tour will be in its fourth year.

West Virginia Fat Tire Festival, Elk River Touring Society, Hwy. 291, Slatyfork, WV 26291, tel.: 304/572-3771. This is fat-tire heaven. Paths and fire roads, small streams and shaded groves greet the spectator and participant in this event. Elk River is six hours from Washington, D.C. Weeklong event, usually June.

Wright Wride, Dayton, Ohio, in early October. I'd think of any excuse to be a part of the Wright brothers, those inventors who sprang from bicycling to flying. The Wright Wride is held in October. In 1992, October 4 marks the 100th anniversary of Wilbur Wright's first tour. The Dayton Cycling Club (c/o 515 Talbott Tower, Dayton, OH 45402) has 1,500 members and is one of the top ten clubs in the country. □

LIFE AWHEEL

It's got to be the going there that's good.
—Harry Chapin, "Greyhound"

Fifteen years ago if someone had said to me, "You're going to bicycle 1,100 miles down Baja and pedal across Iowa five times; you will brave airline regulations and stubborn cardboard boxes, lugging your 18-speed everywhere," I would have thought him mad. Not that I was sedentary; I just hadn't discovered bicycling.

No more. I am one of millions. One of approximately 93 million, to be semi-exact, who, according to the Bicycle Federation of America, commute or travel or ride recreationally on or off road. There's the BMX contingent, those on tricycles, recumbents, tandems, racing machines, and water bikes—wonderfully imaginative versions of ye standard bicycle, courtesy of members of the Human Powered Vehicle Association. Of course I can't forget single-speeds, 5-speeds, track bikes, and those which are yet to come. Folks from two to ninety are buckling on helmets and participating. We're not crazy or exercise obsessed; we just know what the sport feels like.

Bicycling is sweet movement. It's the pleasure of getting where you want with a kind of ease—muscles and mind moving instinctively. Cycling revitalizes that old Latin phrase *carpe diem*, seize the day. Check out the world as you sweep by—blue cornflowers, the warning scree of blackbirds, the curve of a brownstone's steps—bicycling is noticing details and listening to your senses. It's about being in the moment, unencumbered as the sun.

Life on a bicycle is simple. Go from point A to point B. Have fun. Earn a few more calories. Exercise. Feel the wind, rain, and stars (apologies to St. Exupéry) on your face. Meet people of like-minded interests. Swiftly do errands, parking with astonishing ease. Ride without effort. Downhill, for example. Move quietly on trails like a deer. On a bicycle you can always take the road less traveled.

While cycling, I am part energy, part road. I am part of the dirt paths and I am in the meadows I slip by, the red poppies and bright daisies.

Bicycling is the closest I believe I'll ever come to flight (sorry, no jumping out of airplanes for me). When I glide down hills, I am flying. The wind sucks at my knees, hair whips from under my helmet, and I tuck into the handlebars, gripping the top tube with my knees to keep the bike stable.

Poor mythological Daedalus, seduced by the sun and his own hubris soared too high, but I'm solid, just floating fast and far. Fitting that the contemporary Daedalus 88, a seventy-pound human-powered aircraft constructed of carbon fiber, Kevlar, and Mylar, was kept aloft by Greek cyclist Kannelos Kannelopolus on a seventy-four-mile flight over the Aegean Sea from Crete to Greece. Hell, even Orville and Wilbur Wright, who took their bicycle-shop know-how to Kill Devil Hill, North Carolina, evolved parts of their airplanes from the simple bicycle.

The Wright brothers knew bicycling is the smooth whir of wheels, the circle of legs, circles on circles:

wheels, freewheel, crank, feet, hubs. Yes, but cycling also engages the spirit, providing speed, perspective, and a feast of fun. Bicycling rejuvenates the capacity for awe and allows you to forge a private relationship with all you pass through. If you're not bit by the "have to have everything bug," it's minimal equipment—helmet, gloves, shorts, stiff shoes, and of course, bicycle.

In everyday life, there's often much that's not particularly memorable. Traffic drones on without surcease. Bills arrive with disgusting regularity, and the daily dollar shrinks. On the bicycle, the opposite is true, whether the ride is a long-distance excursion or an around-the-neighborhood cruise. All the senses are engaged. Every route has a surprise—a child grinning from a window, the chant of frogs in spring rain, or leaves moving like butterflies in a breeze. It's the feel of air on your skin and making your own pace.

The body, too, is happy. Even if the calves are a tad stiff or a foot complains, mentioning an ache or two, there's a smooth flow, a feeling of belonging as you drift on roads dappled by sunlight, or pass confidently on streets shared by cars. While some rides may show all too clearly in what poor shape you're in, others can be landmark events, when you finish a course in record time or have energy to spare. Everything works together: when you spot a side road or trail hazard, your entire body reacts, checking out options and adjusting, swerving if need be in one direction or another. With practice, bike, body, and brain become one.

If I were encouraging someone else to discover cycling, I'd stack the deck. I'd find a fairly level route, perhaps in a valley with a winding road. There'd be mountains nearby, little traffic, and meadows. If possible, the ride would skirt a lake, providing views at every turn. There would be cattails, swallows, and sunshine. For the first half hour or so, my new cycling buddy and I would spin, pedaling rapidly without pushing hard, and chatting while we warmed up. I'd encourage my companion to keep up his or her cadence, aiming for 90 to 120 rpm (crank revolutions per minute). Then there might be a modest hill or two to grunt up, with a view. Just enough of a hill to feel challenged, not defeated. And then there'd be a downhill, exuberant, with a hint of flying. A good first ride, one to make the new cyclist sing, the earth open up.

Of course, we all can't live near such scenery and terrain, but even a ride in an urban setting can whet the appetite, help someone decide to go for cycling. I relish getting around Washington, D.C., by bicycle, checking out the Lincoln Memorial at sunset and easily avoiding congestion. Why hoard what cycling feels like?

If I could get everyone on a bike, we'd pedal out for a picnic. We'd have a glorious lunch: chunks of crusty bread, glistening Greek olives, and cheese weeping against lush, homegrown tomatoes. No wimpy hydroponically created tomatoes. Not those pale water globes, so mocking of the word *tomato*. We'd have beefsteaks, red beauties picked from the vine.

Cycling demands that. It helps everything be good, actually makes all food wonderful, the fuel for the road. No other way of getting around is so efficient. Figuring that it takes approximately thirty-five calories to fuel one

bicycling mile, what other transport requires merely one banana to get three miles?

Sometimes I think bicycling is all about eating. Hell, often I know this to be so. Take the challenge of a century, a single 100-mile ride. I can recall the views, the valley spreading out, a welcoming hand. Shaped by glaciers, the hills unwind like a slow pitch. Then in lush gardens, there's canteloupe, just beginning to ripen on the vines. Corn crackles in the fields. Imagine it cooking in a pot just some ten or so miles down the road. Or, if the picker can't wait, imagine standing in the center of a field, sinking teeth into its sugary freshness.

Strawberry stands with their red sweetness wafting out, ready to ensnare. Small towns and homemade pies, crusts thick and soft with fruit juices. Sitting out on a porch sipping a lemonade prepared by a couple of kids earnestly trying capitalism. Lemonade at just ten cents a cup, complete with all the free floating lemon bits and questions anyone could ever handle: "Is it tough to bicycle?" "Where do you sleep?" "Want to buy more lemonade?"

Local roadside stands, tomatoes stacked in masses; green peppers, sharp and crunchy; and the occasional pile of plums, purple and sweet, perfect for a quick stop.

Long-distance touring can be days of great food strung together. Of course, there's the understood axiom that practically anything tastes good after hours of cycling. I remember spaghetti miraculously cooked to perfection and coated with a canned tomato sauce enlivened by fresh tomatoes and fresher basil. If the campground was near an ice cream supply, wonderful. Creamy chocolate, swirled in a crisp, graham cone. You had to be quick and

Food

Forget all those articles about forgoing ice cream due to its lack of immediate digestibility. Phooey! It's a hot day. You're under the only shade tree in town with a cold chocolate cone clenched in your left hand. Your tongue is carving symmetrical swirls in the scoops. Indigestion? Unless you're exceedingly intolerant of lactose, I wouldn't even think about it.

Well, I don't eat ice cream all the time, or even for breakfast (except when I'm in Italy). For my first meal of the day, I prefer what I call good carbs—easy to digest, stick-to-the-ribs, and simple to prepare. That leaves instant oatmeal with a bit of honey, whole wheat pancakes, fruit, and some warm beverage. Lunch can be a remarkably easy (and satisfying to me) peanut butter sandwich, fruit, some cut-up veggies, and lukewarm water. I find that really cold drinks—especially on hot days—give me stomach cramps.

Drink before you're thirsty, eat before you're hungry is a rule whose origin I don't know. Follow it. Empty your water bottle every hour on a ride; if it's warm, drink a pint every half hour, at least.

Dinner provides an opportunity for more carbohydrates: the ubiquitous pasta, good bread, and more fruit (or brownies or ice cream). Snacks can be simple dried or fresh fruit, graham crackers, bread or gorp, or food bars.

munch on the crumbling homemade cone, then deftly go for the melting ice cream.

Even peanut butter, that sometimes tiresome stalwart of cyclists and hikers alike, could taste gourmet. I'd mix a spoon of the chunky stuff in with hot instant oatmeal in the morning. Just a little protein to keep me going. Or a bowl of oats sweetened with honey, brown sugar, raisins, or maple syrup. Breakfast could be oatmeal and wild blueberries, small but with a flavor so intense they belied their size.

Still I suppose watermelon will never be quite as sweet or as important as on a hill somewhere on the eighth RAGBRAI, the *Des Moines Register*'s Great Annual Bicycle Ride Across Iowa, my first one in 1979. Two friends and I had eagerly watched scrawled signs posted frequently along a ten-mile stretch, announcing Just Ahead. Ice Cold Watermelon, 50 Cents.

For what seemed to be twenty miles, those signs taunted us; we'd pedal up one hill simmering in Iowa's July heat and crane our necks for that elusive watermelon stop. Then down the next hill we'd swoop, hoping that, plunk, in the middle of this valley, would be what we waited for. This went on until finally there they were. At the top of the next hill, five incredibly enterprising high school students waited. A truckful of striped melons poised. The students were slicing huge chunks out of the melon as fast as they could, accepting our money haphazardly and throwing it, watermelon stained, into a cigar box.

All three of us made a great show of sitting down with our hard-won fruit. There's a photograph that survives:

We are chin deep in watermelon. Black seeds cling to our cheeks and pink juice dribbles down our hands, moving toward our elbows. We look protective of our watermelon and not particularly happy, just tired and intent on the fruit. Watermelon, surely a bicyclist's best summer snack.

Food and friends combine to form memories so poignant they are ropes to other days. Sitting on a hill on my Baja expedition. It's probably day eight of the trip and I am tired, having leaped from my daily routine to pushing the pedals 80 to 100 miles a day. And these are pedals connected to a bicycle burdened with sleeping bag, tent, eight pounds of water, emergency peanut butter, clothes, sunscreen, and more, much more.

Anyway, the view takes in at least ten miles in any direction. It's hot and I'm attempting to sit in the shade of a cactus while spooning some peanut butter. The air rises like fog from the blue land, rippling in the midday sun. Today, like Proust and his famous madelines, a spoon of peanut butter in the heat of day opens that memory like a can. Suddenly Baja and its serene, alien landscape pop into view. I'm lacquered with double-digit sunblock, and fully in Baja. There are no vestiges of Los Angeles, Venice Beach, or any place north of me. There are just some annoying turkey buzzards circling as if they'd be happy with the peanut butter or my slightly fried skin.

A friend scrunched next to me, holding a can of mango juice. Ah, that incredibly sweet, cloying juice: it propelled me through Baja. I returned to Los Angeles with an addiction to it—and the casual habit of looking right, left, and then—if everything was fine—dropping

my black drawers and using the only facilities around.

Sooner or later anyone who ever sits on a bicycle contemplates the open road. It might even be a slender trail, meandering off just over the hill and out of sight. What would it be like to slip down that? To pack up the bicycle for a weekend, week, or longer adventure? Just leave for a while.

I'll just come out and say it. Long-distance bicycle touring is great. Whether you're one who wants to pack a credit card and minimal equipment, hook up with a touring company, or one who delights in portaging the whole works.

Day after day of just cycling. Mountains come into view slowly. There's time to study the way geological forces created faults and uplifts, the ragged peaks towering above cool possibilities. Tons of simple pleasures.

The oddest things are immensely pleasurable. Showers, for example. I've got my private list of the world's top ten showers. One, for example, was surrounded by screaming peacocks flaunting their plumage and sounding like cats in distress. It was just outside of Lassen National Park, and it was my first shower in four days of hard cycling. Ah, hordes of hot water and a warm place in which to dry.

After showers, encouragement ranks high. A friendly wave on a steep hill from a motorist. The woman who held out a jar of grape juice at the top of Logan Pass. Nectar. Meeting another cyclist going in the opposite direction and sharing hints and warnings.

Speed is not of the essence in cycling. Quite the contrary, actually. Witness my touring experience in the

American and Canadian Rockies.

Turtles could probably pass me, I muse, crawling in my lowest gear up Logan Pass. All around me the American Rockies spread their geographical formations, and on my left, bits of shale fall harmlessly to the road. The term for the slow downhill movement of rocks and soil due to gravity is creep, and that's definitely what I am doing uphill. It will take me and the others in my Bikecentennial group a while to push up these twenty miles of six- to seven-percent grade.

Day five of a 600-mile, self-supported (you want it, you carry it) tour from Missoula, Montana, to Jasper, Alberta, in Canada, has brought us this challenge. My leg muscles are becoming more defined each day. I feel like Bill Bixby of the TV series "The Incredible Hulk," my muscles bursting through my shorts. It's no wonder my legs are metamorphizing into "thunderthighs," portaging as they are some thirty-five pounds of clothing, sleeping bag, tent, kitchen equipment, camera, and other miscellanea.

I am as similar to a turtle as possible, not in slowness (see the overpacked cyclist on the downhills!) but in carrying my house with me. We thin-skinned humans need a lot, or believe we do. Traveling by bike necessitates paring. It's good for the soul. Two T-shirts, a set each of arm and leg warmers, bike shorts, a Windbreaker, and a warm sweater. You can only wear so much at one time anyway.

Whatever is needed is fastened to what I propel forward. My front handlebar bag has my camera, several granola bars, which I am rapidly getting tired of, passport, money, sunscreen, insect repellent, and pad and paper. Postcards ready for mailing are wedged in between the stuff. I'm writing joyous, happy notes to everyone revolving in a nine-to-five job.

Far from routine, but making your own clock—that's what long distance travel by bicycle is. While I watch the sunset approach on the Oregon coast, somewhere south of Cannon Beach, people in big cities are getting into crowded trains. Children turn corners sharply, moving closer to home. From here, the world is a wheel and sun and salty air.

The waves along the coast are even, like the children of gods riding sleds. Look, their white faces are upturned. The foam is lacy, like a slip or wild Queen Anne's lace.

Sure, Alaska, Montana, Australia, France, and Scotland are grand places to travel through by bicycle. But wait. The beauty of bicycling is that you don't have to go far for spectacular experiences. Try this:

Bloomington, Indiana, home if the Bloomington Bicycle Club, has its annual Hilly Hundred ride in early fall. Hundreds of cyclists throng to this event, which features a feast after the hills have been conquered. (Beware of geographical nincompoops who insist Indiana is flat.) Tables in the local state park groan under the weight of pasta, brownies, vegetable casseroles, hot bread, and other contributions.

When I attend the Hilly Hundred, the autumnal browns and oranges, the occasional cyclists in red clothes, make me feel as if I'm a double in a painting by Brueghel. All that's missing are the servants and women in white aprons.

Rain

Bicycling in the rain can actually be fun. A well-dressed cyclist can enjoy challenging the elements. An important consideration in wet weather is how differently your brakes will react. In general, wet brakes can take up to four times the distance for a stop in dry conditions. Adjust accordingly; allow yourself time to stop and consider not going as fast.

I'm fond of preventing skunk stripes, that grimy strip of road dirt up the back of your jacket that's kicked up off the rear wheel. A makeshift plastic cover over your rear rack can prevent this. If you're on your mountain bike, consider getting off the trail. Mountain bike advocates believe riding some trails in wet weather can cause damage, something a responsible off-road rider shoud seek to avoid.

As far as clothing goes, I use a jacket with vents or zippers under the arms, a long "tail" in the back, and a roomy hood. The material is breathable, allowing my sweat to make it to the outside world instead of drenching me under the jacket. In cool weather, I'm happiest with a wool shirt or jersey, some sort of neck covering, a rain jacket, wool leggings, rain pants, waterproof booties, and thin gloves over my biking gloves. If it's pouring so hard I can barely see—or raining on top of a slippery surface of leaves, I'll contemplate bailing out. That's a good time to find a local café and test the eats.

While the Hilly Hundred's terrain is memorable, one of my most important rides starts innocently enough on a typical, forty-mile outing with the Bloomington Bike Club. The promise of a drizzle prompts the packing of a rain jacket.

As I cycle through the forest, clouds form in the blue sky, coming together as if for a family reunion. Soon it rains, not heavily, but all-pervasive, soaking my helmet, running down the side of my face and into the neck of my jacket. Water squishes out of my shoes and my shorts. I could not be any wetter if I jumped, fully clothed, into the nearby reservoir.

The woods are close in; densely packed maple and oak trees convey a sense of riding through a damp tunnel. Rivulets of water run across the road, splashing up when my wheel rolls through them. From behind me, my back wheel throws up dirt; I have no rack protector or fender—I can feel a thin stripe of mud forming up my spine, the proverbial cyclist's skunk tail.

Reaching for my water bottle, I drink deeply, tasting particles of grit. Tepid water glides down my throat; warm rain falls into my face, dribbling down my neck and pooling in my jersey. I am water, of water, flowing like the road, the small clear creek next to me. All of my body, which is some 90 percent water, is of this compound. There are no barriers, just a sense of peace. At this moment, I am both connected to the earth and released from it; the wheels of my bicycle and my legs are moving wonderfully unconsciously. I know where I belong.

Sometimes there are moments in our lives—jewels, really—when our often maddening sense of who we are—that rigid ego persistently placing the pronoun *I* in front of everything—disappears. It just fades away. Our skin flies off, dissolves into the universe, and there are no barriers. Our name, conscious anchor that it is, floats away, distant and irrelevant.

And that was how I felt that gray day in Indiana. And that is how I have felt on the bicycle again and again in Montana, California, Vermont and other places; connected to the earth and happy to be there.

Bicycling's beginning goes way back. Way before the auto, light rail, truck, bus, motorcycle, airplane, and other transportation staples of contemporary life. Bicycle-like drawings were among the sketches of Leonardo da Vinci, fifteenth-century inventor and painter extraordinaire. The practical beginning, however, was not until 1817 and the invention of the Hobbyhorse or Draisienne by the German Baron von Drais. This bicycle was a beam on wheels with a primitive, rudder steering mechanism and a padded seat of sorts, and was propelled by pushing against the ground with the feet. The machine attracted considerable interest, but more as a novelty toy for the upper classes than as practical transport on the rough roads of the day.

In the mid-1860s a Frenchman, Pierre Michaux, added pedals to the front wheel and changed von Drais's rudder to handlebars. Michaux's creation was called a velocipede and could weigh as much as 100 pounds. Still, the change to pedal power gave a considerable boost to performance, and technical development was swift. Later models featured ball bearings, frames with spring suspension, and a simple brake. Manufacturing spread from France to Britain and America.

While someone must have challenged a fellow cyclist to drag before 1868, that is the year of the earliest recorded bicycle race. Of course this happened in Paris, quite fitting since the legendary Tour de France, which began in 1903 and is considered the world's most important bicycle race, ends near the Arc de Triomphe. The Tour is a passion of the French and anyone who loves the spectacle of bicycle racing.

I dream of being one among thousands who line the Tour's route, shouting out their favorites' names. I'd root for Davis Phinney, Greg LeMond, Steve Bauer, Dag Otto Lauritzen, Andy Hampsten, Erik Breukink, and maybe Miguel Indurain. I know the most about these racers, having followed part of their cycling careers. (While covering the 1991 Tour Du Pont, I clung to a press motorcycle tailing Steve Bauer during a time trial. On our motorized transport, we could barely keep up with Bauer as the technically difficult course twisted and climbed. What grace, speed, and control that Canadian has.)

Unfortunately, I've missed viewing the cycling prowess of such legendary wearers of the Tour de France's *maillot jaune* (the race leader's yellow jersey) as Eddy Merckx, Bernard Hinault, and Fausto Coppi. I'd love to watch the Tour, preferably in the company of veteran cycle journalists such as Peter Nye and Samuel Abt, whose expert commentary would provide a thorough history of each racer, and place their performances within the complex nuances and rivalries of team strategies.

I'm always amazed at the likes of Davis Phinney, John Tomac, Jeannie Longo, Phil Anderson, and others who've made the bicycle their career and who can move it like no others. Their ability to train, suffer, strive, and win is noble. Strength wells out of them. Every time I've seen Davis Phinney hurtle his bike past the sprint line with a wondrous mixture of stamina, grace, and strength, I know we can fly, at least with the help of a bike.

Over the last twenty years in America, a racer's lot has somewhat improved. In the 1970s racers were a small, elite group. They were also a bit ragtag, with little sponsor support. Some garnered modest stipends and occasional bicycle components or frames. You had to be truly dedicated; few made a living from racing alone. Now it's easier to pay the bills as a professional racer, although pros and amateurs can still struggle. Sponsors are a bit more plentiful. After all, there are more products to advertise and cycle racing is now featured on television.

After the velocipede came the high-wheel bicycle, later known as an ordinary. A spectacularly tall bicycle, with a front wheel between four and five feet high, it was efficient but unstable, and nearly impossible to brake—qualities which made high-wheel riders vulnerable to traveling conditions. Back then, most roads were dirt tracks. When it rained, the roads became swamps, and wheels of all vehicles would bog down. When the sun shone again, the mud hardened into washboards of deep ruts. Cyclists on high bicycles found the going tough. Because the rider was almost straight above the front wheel, hitting a rut or stone could—and often did—mean a quick trip over the handlebars, the dreaded "header."

Enter the British Cyclists' Touring Club (CTC) in 1878, and two years later, its American counterpart, the League of American Wheelmen (L.A.W.). The British organization sought to improve highways and public attitudes. It worked hard at that and at spreading the word, especially across the ocean, to America. Meeting for the first time in 1880 in Rhode Island, a group of some thirty-two bicycle clubs formed the League of American Wheelmen. The organization started the Good Roads movement, which lobbied for better roads. During its heyday, the L.A.W. grew to 104,000 members, due in part to their alliance with farmers, who were also weary of the seasonal impassability of local roads.

Although L.A.W. has gone through various permutations, surviving for several years in an ardent supporter's home, it is still around 111 years after it was founded. Other organizations and groups also have evolved to deal with the challenge of encouraging cycling and cycle-safe roads, routes, and paths. Some are national organizations such as Bikecentennial and the Bicycle Federation of America while others are regionally based, including Transportation Alternatives (New York) and the East Bay Bicycle Coalition (California).

While bicycle organizations in the 1880s were gathering strength, the very shape of the bicycle was itself undergoing welcome modifications. With the advent of the chain drive, the high bicycle gave way to the safety bicycle; two wheels of unequal size became two wheels of same size. The safety, as it was so aptly named, was easier to mount and balance, and could negotiate obstacles without stopping short and cartwheeling the rider.

The safety bicycle became a boon for women. While arguments raged over whether women were even suited for bicycle riding, they quickly took to it. In her book, *How I Learned to Ride the Bicycle*, Frances Willard, president of the Woman's Christian Temperance Union, declared, "She who succeeds in gaining the mastery of the bicycle will gain the mastery of life." That might sound farfetched, but consider the confidence earned from getting around on your own, especially at a time when few women did.

The bicycle offered women independence, companionship, fresh air, and fun. Not surprisingly, it hastened the demise of those heavy soul-confining things that went under the name of clothes—bustles and corsets that robbed whales of their bones and women of easy breathing. Those tight-fitting costumes and bulky skirts evolved into clothes more conducive to movement. Women began to wear scandalous bloomers or culotte-style skirts as a practical alternative to the long skirt. For some, the sight of women cycling alone was sacrilegious enough.

While Margaret Valentine Le Long did wear a skirt, she cycled alone, following railroad tracks from Chicago to San Francisco in her daunting 1896 journey. I wonder what some of those folks who objected strenuously to her trip would think of today's colorful, skintight cycling clothes. Currently, the only rules are to be comfortable and visible.

A mere fifteen years ago, it felt as though women cyclists were few and far between or practically invisible. I remember moving to Clemson, South Carolina, to teach at Clemson University. With an abundance of isolated secondary roads and friendly motorists, the area offered great cycling. The roads skirted large lakes fringed by loblolly pines and red earth. Hills were plentiful—if you wanted them. Kudzu was also in abundance. In bloom, its fruity scent dominated the air.

For three months or so I thought I was the only woman who cycled within a fifty-mile radius. I'd suit up in my helmet, gloves, and black shorts, wishing for a cycling companion. The twenty-two-mile loop I cycled daily demanded a friend with which to share it. Sure, I'd occasionally ride with the guys, but at that time in Clemson, there weren't that many, and they could be downright competitive. Most of them were aspiring racers. My idea of a ride wasn't (and still isn't) to pull out all the stops. I'll sprint for road signs with the best (well, mediocre) of them, but not constantly.

One day while in a car with a fellow cyclist, I spotted what looked to be a female form riding. She had on a helmet and was spinning down the road on some seriously muscled legs. I made the driver pull way ahead of her, and then I jumped out. Waving furiously, I stopped her. We spoke and made plans to cycle together. Micki, also a professor at Clemson, would prove to be a long-term buddy. We cemented our friendship over miles of asphalt, talking about teaching, muscle aches, bad weather, and men. I was happy—a female to share a love of cycling with. In general, being a woman cyclist was such a novelty that you were rarely bothered. Gawked at a bit, however.

No more. Women have their own rides and network, the Women's Cycling Network. There's the WOMBATS (Women's Mountain Bike and Tea Society), and there are more and more female racers. The Ore-Ida ride, not in the European international schedule because the stages are considered too long for women, attracts lots of participants and spectators. Now clothing and bicycles are actually designed for women. There's been a heartening amount of around-the-world female cyclists. Men, too.

In 1984, women's cycling was added to the list of Olympic events. That year Americans Connie Carpenter and Rebecca Twigg brought home the gold and silver, respectively. Theirs was a finish that had a crowd of 200,000 screaming in delight. Marianne Martin also made 1984 a red-letter year for women cyclists. The Tour de France Féminin, newly created for women by Tour de France organizers, had eighteen stages, 620 miles, and Marianne Martin. She became the first American cyclist to win a stage of the Tour, the first to wear the legendary yellow jersey. And when the final stage ended in Paris, Martin was the winner.

The Race Across AMerica (RAAM), a cross-country ultra-marathon challenge, has had its share of female competitors, too. Some, like Susan Notorangelo, Elaine Mariolle, and Casey Patterson, have competed more than once. While the 3,000-odd-mile course varies from year to year, participants can count on grueling miles and often do without sleep. Susan Notorangelo, a mother of two, has crossed the country by bicycle at least seven times. At age thirty-six she won the women's 1989 RAAM (2,952 miles) with a time of nine days, nine hours, and nine minutes. Her husband, Lon Haldeman, is also a cyclist of note. He has held five transcontinental records and has cycled across the country twenty-one times.

Oddly enough, much of what was peculiar to cycling in the 1890s is surfacing again, albeit sometimes in slightly different form. In the 1890s, continuous six-day bicycle races drew thousands of spectators in Madison Square Garden. While the venue is different, these endurance races persist in other forms, including the Race Across AMerica, now in its eleventh year, and Paris–Brest–Paris, another ultra-marathon event. Back in 1895, streetcars in New York had hooks for bicycles. Now various municipalities, including Phoenix, Arizona, are attaching racks to public buses, enabling cyclists to use more than one mode of transportation.

Even putting police on bikes, a concept which has proven immensely successful in many cities, including Seattle, Washington; Tulsa, Oklahoma; and Newark, Delaware, was predated by some ninety years. New York City police commissioner Andrews began a bicycle patrol in 1895. There were others back then who also saw the advantage of bicycle transportation. In the late 1880s, England put members of the Gloucestershire Regiment on bicycles, and in this century the Ho Chi Minh Trail in North Vietnam was used not only by North Vietnamese militia on foot, but also on heavy balloon-tire bikes.

Romance has had a helping hand from the increasingly popular bicycle. Remember "Daisy, Daisy," also known as "A Bicycle Built for Two"? Composed in 1892, it is still sung today. There were side-by-side bicycles, quaint contraptions that enabled couples to bicycle and to talk. Even racers got into the act—one convincing a stubborn sweetheart to marry him after it was certain he'd emerge victorious in a six-day bicycle race in New York's Madison Square Garden.

This determined suitor was Charlie Miller, and it was 1898, day five of a six-day race. Since Charlie had a twenty-mile lead on his nearest competitor, his companion Genevieve Hanson was persuaded he was going to be the victor. Miller finished his six-day, 2,007.20-mile race and leaped into a brand-new racing outfit so that he and Genevieve could be married.

Then there was Diamond Jim Brady, who presented a gold-plated bicycle with an amethyst-studded headset to his girlfriend, singer Lillian Russell.

"Wanted: female cyclist to put in the miles. 50/day on weekends. Optional casual weekday rides. Contact. . . ." To help foster romance, various cycling publications have in-search-of (ISO) classifieds, which are really an athletic twist of the usual classified "personals." Bicycle tours and clubs just for single cyclists have evolved over the years. Hundreds advertise for a new friend to join them on a one-time ride or even on a trip around the world. Even in regular clubs, sharing a love of cycling brings people together. Some couples structure a wedding around the bicycle, riding off into the sunset on a tandem. In addition to romance-friendly tandems, there's a side-by-side cycle called the Honeymooner. Literature on it claims that "no one takes a backseat!" I wonder who does the steering, however.

Frame materials may have evolved, but the shape of Russell's and even Diamond Jim's bicycle just hasn't changed a heck of a lot. Look around. The basic diamond shape of the bicycle—whether it's ultra-lightweight and does service as a racing machine or is of thicker tubing and bouncing around on gravel backroads—has not been altered much. In fact, the safety bicycle has been with us some one hundred years.

Sure, there have been modifications; frames can have different widths of tubing and there are new, nifty materials being used for that tubing. Reclining bicycles, or recumbents, have gained fans, and inventors interested in the potential of all human-powered vehicles have created wondrous machines, many based on the simple bicycle. Pedal-powered craft power over the water or scoot across land. The Gold Rush, a covered recumbent propelled by "Fast Freddie" Markham, set records in 1986, going 65.48 miles per hour for 200 meters.

But as anyone who's ever jumped a curb or skidded into gravel knows, the biggest bicycle news is the mountain bike. The off-road, all-terrain, or mountain bike has evolved rapidly in the last ten years. Whew! It's hard to find anything that's taken off as much as this reinvention of the old balloon-tire bikes of the 1930s. They were very bulky and mostly for kids, but they certainly paved the way for what we ride every day.

Back in the early 1970s, daredevil cyclists in the Marin area of California were going where no cyclist had ever been before. Descending a forest service trail (no small downhill, this: 1,200 feet in 1.8 miles) on what came to be known as Repack Downhill, they jump-started the mountain bike industry. At the same time, down in Santa Rosa, Tom Hillard was organizing Punk Bike Enduro races.

Who could resist? Taking a bicycle off road, bouncing

around gravel, and not caring about rims or other things that on-road riders fretted about was fun, and fun travels. The early pioneer mountain bikers dressed in sturdy simple clothes, like work shirts, cutoffs, and heavy gloves. Folks like Charlie Kelly, Joe Breeze, Tom Ritchie, Charlie Cunningham, Jeffrey Richman, Gary Fisher, and other enthusiastic mountain bikers, playing in northern California and cruising around Crested Butte, Colorado, energized a whole way of bicycling. Charlie Kelly started the *Fat Tyre Flyer*, documenting and encouraging the craze.

My mountain bicycle withstands urban road surprises, swoops down fire trails around Sugarloaf Mountain, and has explored the rugged Western Highway in Belize, Central America. I've borrowed a friend's bicycle and cycled the secluded city trails near Berkeley, California. All settings, as long as they are open to cycling, provide opportunities for bumping about on the mountain bike.

In fall around Maryland's Sugarloaf area, the maples shake their leaves down. Almost everything smells like a fireplace and damp earth. I watch the trail carefully, trying to see if underneath the piles of leaves are deep ruts or anything that will unseat me. But the mountain bike is terribly forgiving. Hit a tree root or bounce awkwardly over some rocks and you can usually remain upright. Just take on the mind-set of an eleven-year-old; the world is dirt and trees and places to play. There's just something about my position on the mountain bike— the upright handlebars—and something about knowing it can withstand much more abuse than a road bike that releases me. Hit a pothole? No worry. There's a big puddle? Go through it, not around it. And make sure you get plenty of dirt on your sneakers.

Even if you've never been off road on your mountain bike, just knowing the spirit of a kid lurks in the bicycle is enough. You just never know when it will emerge. I find city riding particularly fun on my off-road bike. Washington, D.C., streets provide an unending panorama of surfaces and scenes. If I'm not pounding over an intensive quarter mile of potholes, then I'm trying to bunny-hop a deep rut left over from utility digging. On my sturdy (read tank) bicycle, I can relax a bit, enjoy the scene. Cities seem to spawn sidewalk cafes, people hanging out in the open. As I drift by, I too can people-watch and quickly survey the food. Sidewalk sales, especially book markdowns, are immediately accessible. I just pull over and lean over the top tube to see if there's anything I want. Circling around the museums, I get another view of them and can easily stop for a few moments to take in a favorite of mine, the outdoor gardens at the Hirschhorn Museum. Even though I follow all the traffic laws, I progress through the downtown, doing errands, using the Library of Congress, for example, a lot quicker than anyone in a car. And all on a vehicle I know can withstand the rigors of city riding.

Aiding and abetting this off-road explosion has been an improvement of bicycle frame materials. In general, you can get stronger frames for less weight (not less money yet!). My blue bicycle, circa 1960, was all steel, weighing in at an indestructible, earth-bound forty pounds. In those days, bicycles were made of plain, mild steel and were either heavy or heavier. Now there's heat-treated alloy steel, aluminum, carbon fiber, man-

IMBA Rules of the Trail

1.
Ride on open trails only.

2.
Leave no trace.

3.
Control your bicycle.

4.
Always yield trail.

5.
Never spook animals.

6.
Plan ahead.

Bicycle Maintenance

My mountain bike is an archeologist's delight and my road bike is even grimier. Fortunately, bikes are fairly forgiving creatures. Here are a few easy things to do and check weekly. Do them more frequently if you ride hard and often.

Keep your tires properly inflated. Check them for cracking due to wear or heat, and for glass cuts. If they are damaged, replace them.

Clean your chain and lube it. Get a lubricant that does more than clean. You need something with, hmm, excuse me, teeth. If your bicycle has gotten soaked, wipe off the chain and the bicycle thoroughly. Lube immediately to prevent rust.

Make sure your brake pads are properly adjusted and not worn too much. Cables should be taut, without frayed ends. Check that quick-release wheels and/or brakes are fastened properly.

Once a year have a complete overhaul. Repack the hubs, bottom bracket and headset with good grease, replace worn cables and tires, and in all, make the bike gleam. Then go out and get it dirty.

ganese, and titanium. There are frames that weigh less than 2.2 pounds—an entire bicycle can weigh 18 pounds, down from the usual 25.

For every advocate of each material, there are three for the other. In general, a more practical distinction is made between lower-and higher-quality frames. Lower-quality steel frames are heavy, not particularly resilient, and ride that way. Higher quality steel frames are both strong and light. Steel is a well-understood material and is easy to repair—a point to consider if you like riding in out-of-the-way places.

Aluminum is very light, and can be formed into large-diameter tubes, which make lightweight but stiff (e.g., not whippy) frames. On a dollar-per-pound basis, aluminum is a great value. Titanium is the newest goody in the bike store bin of candies. It is both very light and very expensive. People describe the ride as wonderfully smooth and note the material's inability to corrode. There are some mighty nifty-looking titanium frames out there; works of art eloquently gleaming. Then there are carbon fiber composite frames. Carbon fiber is the lightest, stiffest, strongest material of all, and according to testers, rides like a dream.

Overall, you need to consider strength, lightness, durability, rigidity, your cycling needs, and cost. If I'm pedaling up a hill, I want to be on a frame that's strong as well as light; I'm not interested in sacrificing strength for weight. I also want something that won't flex like mad under my power and waste my good energy. I'm not interested in feeling every piece of grit, bump, or rough surface in the road, and I want something that will last, through short commutes, major excursions, bike handlers, and my own erratic maintainance.

My own introduction to frames and materials came when I'd outgrown my first serious bicycle, a mixte frame, and chose to happily invest in something sleeker. My friend Dave shared a few drinks with me at George's Buffet in Iowa City and filled me in. He knew of several companies, the few that actually made small-sized frames. He mentioned custom frames, but at that point, I didn't want the expense of a frame built just for me. In the Iowa heartland it seemed both impossible and exotic. Dave had another view: "Remember"—his voice reflected caution—"are you going to ride seriously?" In other words, after I spent some 500 or so 1979 dollars would I relegate the bicycle to the garage? I didn't know much back then, but I did recognize that bicycling would be my life sport, something to keep my knees supple and my legs firm, way into my nineties. So I dug deep into my pocket and bought a bike that would fit, last, and encourage me onto greater heights. Money was a secondary concern; I wanted a bicycle for life.

Know that it's not just the frame material but the combination of the frame's geometry and fit that provide the ride. The racing bikes I've tried were nimble, sleek, and light. They were made of Reynolds 531, a lightweight alloy steel tubing, and I practically danced up the hills on them. (I haven't tried a titanium frame yet but hear great things about them.) Riding on a racing frame for a long time, however, isn't as comfortable as, say, a sport touring bicycle, also known as a recreational bike. This style is designed for more casual cyclists who

Buying Bikes
and Equipment

To try to tell you what brand of bicycle to buy, which helmet to use, what type of air pump is best, and so on, would be wrong, because my preferences in products are governed by how well they fit me, and how well they suit my particular needs.

Each of us is physically a little different; each of us has different needs. To make sure you obtain equipment that fits you and suits your needs, choose a good bicycle shop and have the employees help you. The experienced and patient advice of pros is crucial.

If you are buying a bike, it is particularly important to do so from a bike shop. If a bike isn't professionally assembled, tested and adjusted by folks who know what they are doing, then even a "best" brand of bike may be a lemon.

go, for example, on long weekend rides.

One of my favorite types of bike, the touring bike, is harder and harder to find. Why would I want one? Well, for cycling long distances and carrying weight, I like a bicycle with a long wheelbase, which simply means that there's usually at least forty inches of distance from one axle to the other. Think of the true touring bike as a chaise longue. Racing bikes, while quick and responsive, have shorter wheelbases and are not as forgiving. They're designed for speed and quick moves.

Wheels are, after the frame, the most important part of the bicycle. Here's where you can save weight and improve performance. Want to feel like a tank? Stick on heavier rims and fatter tires. Want to sleek down? Pare down the weight and width of those wheels, pump up the pressure, and you've got less rolling resistance; you'll float, so to speak. That's why wheels on upper-level racing bikes are light and skinny; in general, the less that hits the road, the quicker you can go.

Punctures are the bane of cyclists, and nowadays many tires use Kevlar, one of Du Pont's contributions to the world of cycling. Kevlar is tough; when the tire is belted with it, there's a strength that helps make it through glass, tacks, and other fun objects. Put a thorn-resistant or new self-sealing tube in there and your tires are practically impregnable.

The whole business of roadside tube changing has been made easier by pumps that can practically fit in your hands, yet still have the oomph of larger pumps. Some folks don't carry a pump, choosing, instead a CO_2 cartridge. This convenience has a price. The newest Bridgestone catalog reports that "a typical discharge . . . releases the same amount of greenhouse gases into the atmosphere as driving a car 100 miles." Note, however, that all the equipment in the world doesn't take the place of training and know-how.

I got my comeuppance on RAGBRAI. Outfitted with a brand-new 12-speed, light wheels with Campagnolo hubs, shiny duds, fresh gloves, new helmet, and attitude that I could just sweep by about anyone (except the racers), I launched myself on the road like the proverbial bat out of hell. Perhaps twenty, maybe thirty miles into that day's mileage, I was zipping along, feeling proud. Suddenly an orange explosion zoomed by my left side. I barely had time to recognize the form. It was a teenager on a very heavy department store bike wearing—on an eighty-degree day—a Day-Glo orange rain suit. He could have easily lost thirty pounds, yet there he was, blowing me away. Ah, hubris. It gets you every time. Still, I comforted myself, believing that by the end of the day surely his inappropriate garb would get him. Surely some chafing at least.

The heavy nylon rain suit that speedy cyclist wore is still around, but lighter, more porous fabrics have become an outdoor staple. Such a relief. What would we have to look forward to if not for the newest gadget or variation on clothing fibers that seem to emerge weekly?

Du Pont seems to be evolving a new fiber every month, guaranteed to do everything but launder itself. First there was Lycra, now there's Cool Max, Supplex, and Micromattique. These are washer-friendly critters, although I still suspect you have to be somewhat anorexic

to really look good in some. Personally, I'm still immensely fond of cotton and wool. The convenient qualities of polypropylene and other synthetics notwithstanding, I enjoy wool's warmth and cuddliness, and find it cuts the chill better than anything. Wool can also go for days without being washed, and it doesn't smell so awful, something many synthetics can't claim. My riding costume of to-the-knee-length T-shirts now amounts to some ninety, in various stages of disrepair and shrinkage. (Every organized bicycle ride or tour I take presents participants with either a T-shirt or a water bottle.)

Head covering is crucial; I learned that early on. Not only would I be persona non grata if I showed up to bicycle with my buddies, sans helmet, but somehow I just wouldn't feel as safe, as confident, hopping down the hills. Yup, brain buckets—what I still call helmets—have surely changed. Much lighter. Thank you, manufacturers. Cooler—thanks to more ventilation slots in the helmet, not the noggin. There's a push on to outfit kids' heads with helmets, and many companies have designed attractive, lightweight, and test-passing helmets. Bell even has one that comes with a turtle stand to help amuse and encourage the newest helmet wearers, young cyclists or cycle passengers.

Years ago, sixteen to be exact, Bell offered the only bicycling helmet. And it was ugly. Christa Shermer, director of public relations at Bell, smiles ruefully at this. She's contemplating a campaign where all those old Bells are returned in exchange for a handsome amount off a new one. Those new ones are spiffy, light-years and pounds away from the original. Helmets in general have gotten downright pretty, sleek and shiny, brightly colored.

There's been additional interest in kids' safety lately, especially as concerns their heads. Much of this has happened in the last five years. Legislators, parents, and other folks are focusing on bicycle education and helmet wearing. For example, California and Pennsylvania mandate that all kids who are under the age of five and a passenger on a bike must wear an approved helmet. Montgomery County, Maryland, has the most comprehensive law in the country: Anyone under the age of eighteen who is a bicycle operator or passenger must don an approved helmet. In Massachusetts and New York, no one under one year of age is permitted to ride as a passenger on bike. Once that small passenger becomes a one-year-old, he or she has to wear a helmet. And in Bidwell Park, located in Chico, California, everyone must wear a helmet. Fortunately, some programs have sprung up to help parents pay for them; legislators sometimes forget that not everyone can afford the laws they enact.

I've been on the scene when a cyclist has fallen without a helmet. Subdural hematomas aren't pretty, or necessary. I've also seen friends bound back on their bicycles, their helmets broken but their heads intact. The National Safe Kids Campaign relates that 75 percent of all cyclist deaths involve head injuries and that nearly 70 percent of all hospitalized cyclists are treated for head trauma. So . . . here comes my admonition: Always wear a helmet. The *New England Journal of Medicine* declares them 85-percent effective. Pretty good odds. After you've bonked your head is when it's too late to wish you wore a brain bucket. (Yes, the one time I left mine hanging off my rear rack for what was only a two-mile quick errand, I took a flier. Who could have foreseen I'd completely lose my balance over a huge patch of damp spilled oil. Moral: accidents happen, practice avoidance techniques in advance but still wear a helmet.)

Saddles, ah, the root of most evil—cycling evil, that is. So many people come up to me, and in earnest dismay confess that they would cycle more, but, they grimace, the saddle, the saddle! I know of what they speak, but that's been addressed by inventors and designers. Ah, Florite, ah Biosoft. Get a saddle that's been injected with some sort of gel or made of a type of yielding material and make sure the saddle itself is at the right height and angle. Then go for it. Do note that my opinion is my own; a saddle that is comfortable for one person may be painful for another. Many cyclists swear by hard, all-leather saddles and don't mind breaking them and their backsides in. You should try the different kinds for yourself, but in any case, use a saddle designed for your anatomy—narrower for men, wider for women. Some saddles are split down the middle to allow adjustment of the width. Another note: those big bruisers of a saddle, à la tractor style with springs and shocks can actually give you grief. Bigger isn't necessarily better; consider chafing.

Bicycle shorts are to me the equivalent of the wheel, the bungie cord, and the answering machine—things I didn't think I needed but now can't do without. When I put on my first pair of bona fide cycling shorts, I thought a racer would blow by me, whispering, "Imposter." Bicycling shorts were for fast riders. Those of us in the stands adopted them slowly, happy to discover the reasons

Cycling in Traffic

In general, be a predictable and alert cyclist. Of course you should wear a helmet and dress in highly visible colors. It's of great importance to follow all traffic laws, signal your intentions and cycle in a straight line. Crossing from side to side or weaving around makes you difficult to pass safely. Watch out for opening car doors, automobiles turning without a signal—indeed anything you would if you were a motorist. Leave headphones and music at home; your ears provide useful clues and can indeed save your life.

Work on controlling your bicycle and feeling confident with your skills. Practice in a stress-free environment, such as empty parking lots or local parks. Be comfortable braking, turning, shifting gears, and going with the flow of traffic. You might consider using streets that have parked cars. This often leaves a space in the lane that is just bicycle sized. Always scan in all directions and be able to do this without changing the direction in which you are riding. I try to make eye contact with drivers, but I do not count on this to ensure that they see me. It's inevitable that someone will turn in front of you suddenly or simply not see you. (Motorcyclists have long been familiar with this problem.) Resist universal gestures or screaming at the offender; rarely does this help, although I admit I've given in to that impulse more than I'd like to.

racers wore them. Besides, what else did I have that was so handy to wipe all that black chain grease on?

I could have deposited chain lube on my shoes, but they were already giving me grief. Bicycle shoes—well, almost all shoes—have always been the bane of my existence. Years ago, I had a choice of sneakers or pencil-thin torture machines, sleek and made for tiny-footed racers from Italian leather. If I wanted the welcome stiffness of a shoe designed for cycling I had to suffer for it. Not anymore. A shoe fetishist today can indulge, go bonkers. Especially with some of the newest racing versions with a solid carbon fiber sole and foam to absorb shock. Then, of course, there are clipless pedals with freefloat; the float allows your feet and thus your legs to rotate, helping to eliminate the potential of knee damage from feet fixed in the wrong position.

Bicycle gloves now have more options. I can pick ones with gel in the palm, designed to relieve constant stress on the ulnar nerve. (Of course, moving your hands from one position to another is also useful.) I can put thick winter gloves on or make my hands fluorescent arrows. And for someone who signals her intentions in traffic, a splash of color on the hand is helpful.

Shifting mechanisms have gotten lighter, stronger, more able to leap buildings in a single bound. I've got bar-end shifters on my touring bicycle and top-mounted shifters on my mountain bike. Some folks think they're completely archaic, because they're—gasp—not Shimano Index Shifting, the highly touted SIS system that clicks and lets you know how much to move the lever to shift. But I'm happy with them. It's not that I don't think SIS is the next best thing to tubes that heal themselves, it's just, well, I'm happy with what I've got.

Innovations galore. Profile handlebars pitch you more forward, providing a more aerodynamic position and greater comfort over long distances. Heat-treated rims for high-fatigue strength and lightness. Wheelsmith, these wonderful builders in California, have a wheel that's called the Propeller and looks just like that or a steering wheel. The aerodynamic rim is made out of a new composite called Optomium, which is silicon carbide and aluminum compressed together. No broken spokes here.

Then there are those handy, dandy microchips happily sitting on your handlebars. Bicycle computers and then some—doing everything but yell at you to get on the bike and ride. You can get the number of calories burned, distance, cadence, and exotic stuff like power output and chain pedal force. I like computers; they keep me honest. Even when I'd like to think I'm doing at least sixteen mph, they tell me, "No, you lazy bum, you're barely breaking thirteen mph." When the distance seems unusually long or the landscape remarkably similar, I pace myself using the computer. Heart-rate monitors are becoming more popular; they can help you get an optimal workout.

Shock absorbers are the newest rage. These range from relatively simple mechanisms that allow the handlebars to pivot, absorbing impact through a rubber or elastomer bushing, through to bikes with complete suspension systems, shock absorbers front and rear, adjustable for the cyclist's weight and riding style. Of course, the human body is also an effective suspension system; the way you sit on your saddle determines how your built-in shocks—the spring/give in your elbows, wrists, knees, and derriere—contribute. Tires are a form of shocks as well.

I like cycling in the evening. Usually, it's quieter, and when it's balmy, the night air surrounds like a cushion. I pedal like a shadow through neighborhoods settling into sleep. Lights warm windows and toys sprawl on lawns. An occasional dog barks, my lights catch the eyes of cats prowling their boundaries. Everything softens.

When I ride through the city at night, I feel swifter, am an urban swallow. I do avoid certain areas and aim for routes with parked cars, which provide an "alley" for bicycles. When properly lit up, I feel safe. I know, of course, that while riding at night is 20 percent riskier than during the day, I can minimize the danger by making myself highly visible. No black clothing or relying on reflectors. The key is to be seen and to be able to see.

There are numerous options to those pesky generator lights of decades ago. Bright halogen lamps can provide beams that are visible up to 1,500 feet or more. Velo-Lux, for example, has a system that throws a beam 50 to 60 feet in front and about 7 feet wide. When complemented by reflective clothing or vests, reflectors, and a host of flashing lights, I can be a moving light show. This is good. Use all this new equipment to establish a good road presence. A good system will cost around $100, but is worth it.

In Montana, during a full moon, cyclists drive up from Missoula to ride Going to the Sun Highway. My friend Linda speaks of the quiet and the small twinkling lights weaving their way up to the top. There are no cars, just the gentle whir of wheels finding their way by light of moon and halogen bulbs.

It seems impossible that only fifteen years ago there were only two state rides (at least that I knew of): TOSRV (Tour of the Scioto River Valley, starting in 1962) and RAGBRAI (the *Des Moines Register's* Annual Great Bicycle Ride Across Iowa), which will celebrate its twentieth anniversary in 1992.

Forget it today. There are tens and tens of long-distance state rides, and if you think you know your state, think again. Only after you've toured it by bicycle can you begin to make that statement. Clubs are grand opportunities to socialize, discover routes, and make a diffference. With 4,800 members, the Cascade Bicycle Club in Seattle, Washington, is the largest in the country. They run the popular Seattle-to-Portland Ride (STP for short) and support a full-time education coordinator. Potomac Pedalers Touring Club in the metropolitan Washington, D.C., area offers a whole array of rides, for cyclists of all interests and levels.

Over the last twenty years, I've seen a host of organizations come into being to support and encourage bicycling. The Bicycle Federation of America, Bikecentennial, Southern Bicycle League, Rails-to-Trails, and a long list of strong regional clubs augment the list. Bikecentennial is an interesting organization, literally starting in a tent in 1972. Their coming-out-of-the-tent year was 1976, when 4,000 cyclists pedaled on the Transcontinental Route; some 2,000 completed the 4,500-mile trail. Among other achievements, Bikecentennial has mapped 18,000 miles of route, helped develop cycling education programs, and trained bicycle coordinators and engineers. They also design some wonderful cycling T-shirts and hats with big grinning teeth.

Sometimes I believe bicycles still suffer from an attitude that they are nothing but toys for children. Back in the 1930s, everything seemed directed at the younger market. Bicycles were for delivering messages, newspapers, or groceries. Even then, however, they were designed to give the feel of a car. Some, like the Elgin made by Sears, had a fake gas tank. Of course bicycles are for children, but they're for anyone, at any age. Adults will be sorely impoverished if they feel that way.

On the other hand, it's possible to take cycling too seriously. You don't need an ultra-lightweight frame, disk wheels, and profile bars to enjoy riding a bike. When I began to be interested in bicycling, cyclists seemed simpler, that's for sure. Less techno-wienie. Smaller groups, and it was harder to find serious cyclists. We wore big, baggie T-shirts and had nary a thought of fashion. A helmet was a mark of a truly dedicated cyclist.

I've been changed by the last fifteen years of equipment improvements, but not radically. On any given day, I'll pedal off with helmet, shoes, cotton T-shirt, gloves, Gore-tex jacket, and bike shorts. It doesn't take much more than that. I'm certainly grateful for improved saddles, though; when I first started I stupidly had an uncomfortable plastic seat, possibly no more cozy than those on the Draisienne some 150 years ago.

Cycling is essentially a simple pursuit. My friend Steve, a marathon runner and avid cyclist pounding the terrain of New Mexico, lauds the simplicity of his bicycle, ruefully comparing it to the complexities of modern romance. Steve writes, "Relationships are so complicated. Guess that's why I like my bike so much. Give it a new set of tires and a bit of grease every now and then and it's content. Life should be so easy."

Technology? Dan Buettner, bicycle traveler extraordinaire, said of his 12,888-mile Soviet trip, that shoe goo was one of the most important things he carried. It helped keep tires (of which he and his three companions used seventy-three) and shoes together, two essentials any way you look at it.

Too Tyred Tour, three cyclists who put a mere 45,000 miles on their bicycles during a six-and-a-half-year expedition, swore by some things you'd expect and some you wouldn't. Imagine carrying a brazing rod and flux in case of catastrophes or designing a sewing kit capable of handling tent zippers, panniers, and clothing repairs. All those things and more helped the three during their cycle tour of 45 countries, including Nepal, Chile, and Kenya. Two of the three now work for Life-Link International (Box 2913, Jackson Hole, WY 83001, tel.: 800/443-8260), which designs bicycle products based on their worldly experiences. It's technology, but simple and obviously well-researched.

I'm happy to see the numbers of cyclist adventurers and recreational cyclists increasing. The 1890s have been called the golden years of cycling. Thousands watched six-day races and belonged to L.A.W. Racers such as Major Taylor, the first black cyclist, captured the nation's interest and imagination. Bikes connected with trains and trolleys, extending the transportation network. Families went for rides together. In short, bicycling was a part of the nation's consciousness.

It sounds like what's happening today—the 90s, only this time the *1990s*, energizing an interest in all aspects of cycling, including the mountain bike and other equipment. I'd like to think this new golden age will be around longer than a decade; I'd like to believe we can make it happen.

RESOURCES
Helpful Organizations

Whether you are cycling across the country or overseas, the following organizations can provide information and in some instances, connect you with travel-minded folks eager to provide a simple place to stay. Check also Bikecentennial's Cyclist's Yellow Pages (has great listings for overseas maps) and L.A.W.'s Hospitality Guide.

American Youth Hostels, National Office, P.O. Box 37613, Washington, D.C. 20013-7613, tel.: 202/783-6161.

Canadian Hosteling Association, 333 River Rd., Vanier City, Ontario, K1L 8B9, Canada, tel.: 416/368-1848.

U.S. Servas Committee, 11 John St., Rm. 706, New York, NY 10038, tel.: 212/267-0252. International volunteer organization whose goal is to provide opportunities for various cultures to meet.

British Servas Committee, 77 Elm Park Mansions, Park Walk, London SW10 0AP, tel.: 071/352-0203.

Cyclists' Touring Club (CTC), Cotterell House, 69 Meadrow, Godalming, Surrey GU7 3HS, England, tel.: 048 68 7217. □

Maps

There's been a veritable explosion of maps and ride books designed just for cyclists. Many of them are available through your local bicycle or outdoor-recreation store. Others are published and distributed by area bicycle clubs. Some states, Massachusetts and Maryland, for example, have tourism offices that promote bicycling through special maps. These state-funded sources of information usually have a toll-free number, which can be obtained through information.

In addition to the above sources, Bikecentennial publishes excellent maps to accompany the more than 18,000 miles they've researched. The Touring Exchange publishes a catalog listing maps available from other cyclists. There's always your local AAA, whose maps are surprisingly good for bicycle travel. Members of the League of American Wheelmen can avail themselves of volunteers who can suggest routes. Don't overlook word of mouth, either. Other cyclists will often share their best rides. If you're journeying off road, check with local land managers. Always ride where it's legal. In general, do as Robert Frost wrote, "and take the road less traveled."

Bikecentennial, P.O. Box 8308, Missoula, MT 59807, tel.: 406/721-1776.

League of American Wheelmen, 190 W. Ostend St., Ste. 120, Baltimore, MD 21230, tel.: 301/539-3399.

The Touring Exchange, Box 265, Port Townsend, WA 98368, tel.: 206/385-0667. □

Touring Companies

There are tons of touring companies out there. In the company of experienced guides, you can bicycle in Sweden, Michigan, Tasmania, and even Tibet. Some tour companies design trips that meander from inn to inn. Others mix camping with hotels, while several offer camping-only tours. Some tours blend bicycling with white-water rafting, hiking, canoeing, and even ballooning.

Many offer the option of renting a bicycle and may even pick you up from the airport. You can find guides who will cook your every meal and even set up your tent. Other companies invite client participation: be prepared to enjoy stirring a stew or helping to clean up. Many companies focus on structuring maximum interaction with the people whose country or state you are visiting.

If you are new to bicycle touring, you may find it comforting to go first with a company before striking out on your own. The list below represents just a brief smattering of tour companies. Write or call them for further information. Check out the back of various bicycle magazines, *The Bicyclist's Sourcebook* by Michael Leccese and Arlene Plevin, or special issues of *Bicycle USA* (L.A.W.) or *Bike-Report* (Bikecentennial).

American Youth Hostels, National Office, P.O. Box 37613, Washington, D.C. 20013-7613, tel.: 202/783-4943.

Backroads Bicycle Touring, 1516 5th St., Berkeley, CA 94710-1713, tel.: 800/BIKE-TRIP, 415/527-1555.

Bicycle Holidays, R.D. 3, Box 2394, Middlebury, VT 05753, tel.: 802/388-BIKE.

Bikecentennial Tours, P.O. Box 8308, Missoula, MT 59807, tel.: 406/721-1776.

Bike Events, P.O. Box 75, Bath, Avon BA1 1BX, England, tel.: 0225/310859.

Breakaway Vacations, 164 E. 90th St., #2Y, New York, NY 10128, tel.: 212/722-4221.

Butterfield & Robinson, 70 Bon St., Toronto, Ontario M5B 1X3, tel.: 800/387-1147.

Ciclismo Classico, P.O. Box 2405, Cambridge, MA 02238, tel.: 617/628-7314.

Peter Costello, Ltd., P.O. Box 23490, Baltimore, MD 21203, tel.: 301/685-6918.

Country Cycling Tours, 140 West 83rd St., New York, NY 10024, tel.: 212/874-5151.

Easy Rider Tours, P.O. Box 1384, E. Arlington, MA 02174, tel.: 800/488-8332, 617/643-8332.

PAC Tour, P.O. Box 73, Harvard, IL 60033, tel.: 815/943-3171.

REI Adventures, P.O. Box 88126, Seattle, WA 98138, tel.: 800/622-2236, 206/395-7760.

Rocky Mountain Cycle Tours, Box 1978, Canmore, Alberta T0L 0M0, Canada, tel.: 800/661-2453 (U.S.), 403/678-6700.

Touring Exchange, Box 265, Port Townsend, WA 98368, tel.: 206/385-0667.

Vermont Bicycle Touring, Monkton Rd., Box 711, Bristol, VT 05443, tel.: 802/453-4811. □

Long-distance Packing

Mere suggestions for what to take. Remember to spread out everything you plan on taking and weed out half. Less is more. More is too much.

Bicycle Equipment
bungie cords or strap
handlebar bag
lock and cable
panniers
pannier covers
pump
rearview mirror
water bottles, (two or three)
lighting system (or flashlight)

Camping Equipment
ground cloth
pad
sleeping bag
stakes, extra
tent
tent patches

Clothing
arm warmers
bathing suit
bandanna (one or two)
helmet
cycling shorts (two or three)
lightweight non-cycling clothes
gloves, cycling and warm

rain jacket and pants
leg warmers or long cycling pants
sandals or flip-flops
shirt, long-sleeved
shoes, pair for cycling and walking
socks, warm and lightweight
warm jersey or vest
short-sleeved shirts
underwear

First Aid

prescription medication
pertinent medical information
aspirin
bandages
first-aid creme
insect repellent
lip balm
moleskin
sunscreen (wear on any length ride)
tweezers
water-purification tablets or Giardia filter

Kitchen

aluminum foil
can opener (if not a part of your pocketknife)
cup and plate
food (always have an emergency stash of instantly edible stuff)
fuel
matches, waterproof
pot

primer for stove

scouring pad and multipurpose soap (dishes, clothes)

snacks (chocolate!!)

spices (in handy film canisters)

stove

utensils

Miscellaneous

address book (in plastic)

camera and film

compass

cord

copy of your prescriptions

extra glasses or contact lenses

fanny pack or small backpack

flashlight and extra batteries

notebook and pens

maps

passport or other identification

plastic bags

pocketknife (the familiar Swiss Army standby
or some facsimile)

stamps

stuff sacks

sunglasses

tape, tough (electrical, etc.)

traveler's checks

money

watch

Personal

razor
sewing kit
shampoo
soap
toilet paper
toothbrush and toothpaste
towel (small)
comb / hairbrush

Tools

Allen and spoke wrenches
extra brake pads
cables, gear and brakes
chain lube
chain tool
crescent wrench
freewheel remover
hand cleaner
needlenose pliers
nuts and bolts
patch kit
pocket vise
pump
screwdriver
spokes, extra ones
tire, fold up
tire irons
tube, at least one spare ☐

BICYCLING INTO THE FUTURE

The bicycle is a vehicle for revolution.
—Daniel Behrman, *The Man*
Who Loved Bicycles

There are people poking along on bikes near China's Great Wall, and gasping for air as they explore Nepal, Tibet, above 12,000 feet, where the oxygen thins to a few measly molecules.

Down below, on other continents, at lower elevations, mere mortals sidle up to traffic lights, take their chances in the more polluted atmosphere of big cities like New York and London. They're pedaling to work or making a living as couriers. Others, myself included, combine exercise, errands, and easy parking, doing grocery shopping and more by pedal power. Or we cycle off on welcome vacations, exploring local vistas and valleys, leaving aggravation behind. On isolated country roads, we forego maps, packing compasses to navigate the open spaces, the long straight fields.

Anywhere you go—even the Arctic—there's someone with two wheels and a chain, pedals, and brakes, and the belief in two-wheeled fun and function. Associations, industry—hell, even local and federal governments—are getting into the act. Numerous municipalities are putting stripes on the roads for bike routes, adding Share the Road signs with the painted symbol of a bike. They all know a good thing when they see it, even if some need a bit of prodding.

There will always be the bicycle, basically unchanged and natural, a form that functions to perfection. This is something I stubbornly believe. Worthy of great respect (and giver of great delight), this human-powered machine is intrinsic to a livable world. For everyone from the very young to the old, there's a place for the bicycle in all aspects of daily life.

It's easy for me to conjure up what may happen with the bicycle in the next few months, years, and even decades—harder to predict with certainty. But then there are many cards on the table, many people in the picture with wondrous ideas and visions. Still, it's neat to reflect on what the future of cycling could hold. Sure, there will be tons of technological improvements—fabulous new clothing materials, stronger yet miraculously lighter frames, and things as yet undreamed of. But I suspect what will really make cycling fun will be improved services and places to bicycle. I believe bicycling's outlook to be tied to something no less than the health of the planet and the people who live on it.

So down to brass tacks and imagination. We cyclists have heaps to look forward to. The Bicycle Federation of America estimates 1.3 million Americans take cycling vacations. Strength and encouragement in numbers, I hope. Just contemplate the attraction to people looking for family-oriented activities or concerned with fitness. Factor in the popularity of mountain bikes and the interest in environment-friendly transport, and I'd say the future looks like it's got two wheels in it—everywhere you go.

Families are finding bicycling an ideal sport. People can team up on tandems, and children can readily participate. Whether a child is in a carrier mounted on the bike, snug in a trailer, or a partner on a tandem or triplet, there's a way to involve him or her. Dennis Young of Burley Design Cooperative sees a doubling of interest in bicycle trailers in the last ten years. Most families were "athletically active before they had kids," he says. "Now they're looking for the best way to continue, and the trailer provides the means."

Tandems, too, are part of the family cycling picture. I love them—two-fers, twicers, long bikes, or whatever. Going it by tandem can double the fun; it's also a great way to accommodate cyclists of different strengths. Are you ready to go fast and to either captain or stoke a long bike? As stoker, can you happily stare at someone's rear and/or back for hours on end? Now, can you do that *and* not give into mischief (i.e., stuff ice cubes down a jersey or unmercifully tickle the captain)? Or can you be the captain, handle the braking and steering responsibilities while trusting that the person behind you won't give in to overly playful impulses?

I've always been in the stoker position but restrained myself from too much vandalism. There's such a feeling of power on a tandem; two engines instead of one. Downhill speeds are awesome, that's why those bicycles built for two need powerful brakes. Going up hills is one of the few places a single rider can catch a twosome; hills also present a challenge to most tandemers. Don't overlook the treat of having a partner, a sort of Siamese twin cyclist, if you will. You can bet that the mid-1990s will have more and more tandems on the market.

Sometimes you can glimpse a bicycle "semi," a tandem pulling a trailer. Nationwide clubs sponsor tandem-only rallies and rides; a good number of these tandems sport a parent-child team. Add American Youth Hostels and its forty local councils, which discovered that more families want to travel and bicycle together. Near Spencer, Iowa, on my fifth RAGBRAI, I met a family of four pedaling across the country on two tandems. They'd started in Oregon and were aiming for Boston. Each parent captained a bike and had a daughter for a stoker. When I met them, both children, ages eleven and eight, were content, eating ice cream and dribbling it on their parents' shirts. Apparently some 2,000 miles into the ride, there had been no major mayhem.

It doesn't take a psychic to predict that big rides, especially cross-state rides, will boom. Those already in existence, such as Cycle Oregon and BRAT (Bicycle Ride Across Tennessee), are growing phenomenally. Others are too popular. To preserve the quality of the experience (and handle the hordes), participants are limited on such legendary rides as RAGBRAI and TOSRV. Cyclists are also finding it fun to pedal for charity, raising money for a cause while spinning their wheels. It's sort of festive, an athletic, feel-good happening.

Thousands are also seeking bicycle education for their kids. In Missoula, Montana, all fourth-graders receive ten hours of bicycle education. North Carolina has also instituted a bicycle education program. Interest in preventing injuries of all types has given rise to the National Safe Kids Campaign, which also concerns itself with encouraging helmet wear.

What's happening because of these numbers? Well, the federal government and various cities and states are recognizing the place the bicycle has as a recreational and commuting vehicle. The U.S. Department of Transportation has hired a bicycle-pedestrian program manager. Institutionalizing such positions can mean better facilities nationwide. The program manager is Josh Lehman, longtime activist and true friend of the bicycle—expect to find increasing provisions for bicycles in all states' plans.

What sort of provisions? Let's dream. Imagine a twelve-foot-wide path that you can count on as yours. It has lights, a consistently smooth surface, well-marked, safe intersections, and other amenities. On the highways, imagine driver education programs that teach drivers about the rights of cyclists. And traffic laws mandating, for example, that drivers must yield the right of way to bicyclists. How about buried loop detectors that can sense when a cyclist is waiting for a light? Envision bridges that provide a space for cyclists, not urging them (by omission) to hitch or swim across or forget it. Or would you be happy with a well-engineered way across, under, or above the existing system of heavily used freeways and boulevards? How about nationwide programs that teach cycling, encouraging safe, predictable bicycling behavior? Or routes that enable you to cycle directly to school, work, or store? Would you like safe bicycle parking facilities?

When *Prevention* magazine ran an editorial, "Make America More Walkable," which also queried folks about their bicycle needs, more than 500 people responded. Many were angry. In their letters to the U.S. Department of Transportation, they told of fear and frustration, simply trying to walk or bicycle across town. Young and old, they complained about a road system that was designed solely for autos, making other forms of transport unnecessarily difficult and often dangerous.

A few American cities have already set up bicycle-friendly systems worth emulating. If you visit Seattle (don't move there, locals will implore), bring or rent a bicycle and pedal down the popular twelve-mile Burke-Gilman Trail, a handy route for cyclists to get to work or school. A 1987 study has shown that property near the trail is popular, too; values increased six percent. Seattle has full-time bicycle program staffers who are continually helping to improve the bicycling there. Goals include completing a three-mile missing link to Sammamish River Trail, completing a twenty-seven-mile trail. Seattle will also work on the street system, creating more space in the road for bicycles. They envision a bicycle boulevard, à la Palo Alto, California. Is it any wonder people call Seattle a very livable city?

What makes a city, village, or town more livable? For many, it's the overall quality of life—easy access to work, stores, school, and other amenities, such as parks and art events. Several award-winning towns—Seascape, Florida, for example—are cited because of the ease in which people can get around *and* the secondary position in which autos are placed. Livablity, for some, means being in an environment that is sensitive to the needs of pedestrians and cyclists, an environment that actually encourages alternatives to the automobile and has paths that connect people, not roads to divide them. The result can be less traffic in downtown areas, pleasant pedestrian and bicycle thoroughfares, and safe places for children to bicycle. Trails and bike paths tend to encourage folks to get out on their bikes. They feel safer.

Palo Alto, California, long touted as a city friendly to cyclists, has grates that won't trap bicycle wheels and traffic signals sensitive to cyclists. There's a two-mile bicycle boulevard. (Park your cars, they're not allowed.) There are cycle routes along the streets and ample bicycle-parking facilities.

Innovators can look to Europe for additional suggestions. Michael Replogle, president of the Institute for Transportation Policy and Development (ITDP), cites Copenhagen, Denmark, for its "incredible network of paths and arterial streets . . . which were put in over the last fifteen years, resulting in an increase of the percentage of bike trips from 20 to 30 percent." There's also Hannover, Germany, with a population of 800,000. In that good-sized city, over 30 percent of all trips are made by bicycle. Many other European cities offer a fine network of bikeways that penetrate into the heart of city center.

Cyclists have the same rights to the roads as cars, but often those roads are daunting to cyclists, due to the huge amount of car traffic. In the United States, Los Angeles is now planning a four-lane bike path that will go over Wilshire Boulevard and the San Diego Freeway, both of which currently separate bicyclists from neighborhoods.

Boulder, Colorado, has mountains, Connie Carpenter and Davis Phinney and other world-renowned cyclists, and an attitude. In short, bicycles are part of the scene. Currently, 10 percent of Boulder's trips are made by bike;

the city fathers and mothers are working to encourage more. In the typical American city, 2 to 3 percent of all trips are made by bicycle.

Elsewhere, the bicycle assumes a larger role in transportation needs. The Netherlands, for example, is famous for its use of bicycles. In a country half the size of Maine there are over 8,000 separate bike paths, or *fietspads*. Some are parallel with streets and roads, with special bicycle-only traffic lights at junctions. Others stretch through open fields and forests, often going where there are no roads— or cars. You can reach anyplace in the country by bike.

In other densely populated European cities, motor vehicle traffic is calmed with measures such as "sleeping policemen"—humps in the road that cars must negotiate slowly—to make neighborhoods more pleasant, and to encourage cycling. In countries such as Denmark, every road and street in the country has an adjoining bike path.

We in North America tend to lose sight of the fact that not every society is so "auto-centric." Worldwide, there are some 800 million bicycles. Cars are outnumbered two to one. In China, India, Germany, Denmark, and elsewhere, bicycling is an integral part of the transportation system. According to Marcia Lowe's Worldwatch paper, *The Bicycle: Vehicle for a Small Planet*, China has some 300 million bicycles, and "at one intersection, the city of Tianjin [China] counted more than 50,000 bicycles in one hour."

In Nicaragua and Haiti, health and education workers employ mountain bikes to reach clients on rocky rural roads. Bikes Not Bombs, an organization that helps that effort in both countries, is also active in Mozambique,

Commuting

Bicycle commuting doesn't require special equipment, although certain products will make it easier. All you need is a bicycle (no surprise here), helmet, good locking system, and way to carry a change of clothing. Taking some extra time to scout out a route is also useful. In most cases, once you get off the car track, you'll find acceptable—even enjoyable—alternatives to heavily trafficked roads.

Some commuters use a favorite clunker, or old, sturdy bike that's somewhat immune to potholes and rough handling. I've got a lighting system on mine and carry a tool bag, plus two locks (one U-shaped lock with a cuff and one cable lock), which I securely fasten to an immovable, uncuttable object.

In the past, I've gotten by wrapping my clothing around a towel and shaking them out vigorously when I arrived. I then use the towel and some powder to freshen up. I've happily discovered something called the Bicycle Garment Pannier, put out by Eccosport (41 Sutter St., Ste. 1836, San Francisco, CA 94104, tel.: 800/235-3226), which can carry anything, especially wrinkle-prone clothing. This is done in a specially designed pannier that also doubles as a regular garment bag. Then I use my regular pannier, a Specialized one, which fits nicely and is aerodynamic. I also carry a rain jacket (remember, if you have it—cross your fingers—you will be less likely to need it).

one of the world's poorest countries. There the bicycle is a valuable resource, dramatically reducing the time needed to get to places by walking or taking overcrowded and unpredictable buses. Even the Peace Corps has switched some of its volunteers over to mountain bikes.

In North America, the overall value of easily powered and energy-efficient bicycling is slowly reentering the nation's consciousness. Commuting by bicycle, that's the ticket. When I worked in downtown Washington, D.C., I'd snake my way through Rock Creek Park. The path was always busy; tens of people wearing everything from a full suit of Lycra to a conservative power suit with the obligatory tie would zip along. Around the National Zoo, I'd take a detour to see what the ducks were doing in their ponds. All of us heading to the heart of the empire for a day at our computers would move smoothly on the Rock Creek conduit, like fish in a small stream. We got fresh air and a front-row view of dogwoods and cherry blossoms. The prepared had a spiffy lighting system and rain gear, just in case. How simply we got to work, how quickly we parked. Some could change in a local gym or handily had a locker facility in their building's basement. Others, myself included, packed some talcum powder and a towel, sufficient for all but the most beastly D.C. days. A lucky few had guarded bicycle-parking facilities.

When I lived in Venice, a beach community of Los Angeles, the only time I couldn't do my twenty-four-mile-a-day bicycle commute was when the smog was bad. On those days, I'd give up my fifty-five-minute going-there and one-hour return bicycle ride for my small car. Instead of zipping down Venice Boulevard, crossing over on Beverly Glen and practically holding my breath for a hair-raising 100 feet on Sunset Boulevard to Beverly Glen, I'd drive. Driving took twenty to twenty-five minutes one way, depending on traffic. For a mere thirty minutes more, I'd get exercise, a mild sweat (I never pushed it), and great mileage. The return trip was a way to unwind, to cruise down San Vicente Boulevard by the palm trees and hang a left onto Ocean Boulevard. For two miles, I had the ocean on my right. On Wednesdays I'd stop by the Santa Monica farm market, filling my panniers with lettuce, avocado, sprouts, cheese, and calla lilies. I'd feel French, cycling back with flowers propped up against a loaf of bread in my pannier. However, when the air quality was unhealthy or downright hazardous, I ended up driving a car and being part of the problem. Ironic, I know, but high ozone levels made me—and millions—cough. My eyes stung, my lungs hurt, and I just didn't feel comfortable strenuously exercising. And that's what experts advise: when the air quality is bad, and it's usually worse in late afternoon, avoid outside exercise.

Most Americans live within five miles of work, an easy bike ride. Yet currently less than 3 million commute on a daily basis out of a possible pool of approximately 97 million. So what would we say we need to get us commuting? A Louis Harris poll commissioned by *Bicycling* magazine found that 49.3 percent would commute more if there were safe bike lanes on roads and highways. Another 44.5 percent said they'd need financial incentives from employers, while 43.5 percent would commute if there were showers and secure bike storage at work. As *Bicycling* magazine's senior editor Nelson Pena pointed out, "Much of mainstream America is ready for bicycle commuting. The only thing holding it back is a lack of bike lanes, showers at work, and other basic amenities."

If you build it, they will come, as they say in Iowa and elsewhere.

They'll also gather for mountain biking. Amazing to consider that when frame builder Gary Fisher built 165 bikes in 1979 he garnered 85 percent of the market share. For 1991 he manufactured 45,000 frames—a fraction of the 6 million mountain bikes sold that year in the United States.

Most mountain bikers stick to the streets, only occasionally dabbling in off-road riding. As a result, city bikes (or hybrids) are winning converts. This cross between a road bike and a mountain bike offers a comfortable, upright position, lightweight full-size wheels, and other features, making it ideal for gentle off-road riding and not-so-gentle in-town tours. Bicycle manufacturers promise to keep on tinkering with derailleurs, frame weight, seats, hell, everything about mountain bikes.

Technology may be spurring interest in mountain biking, but it doesn't do squat for places to ride. What's the use of having a magnificent mountain bike if you can ride it only on concrete? The boom in mountain bikes and the increased number of riders led to conflicts with other wilderness-area users, and many trails and areas were closed to bikes. Now equestrians, cyclists, hikers, and walkers are seeking to cooperate with one another and share existing open space. After all, minimizing user conflict is only part of the game. Once land is developed, it's taken out of recreational use entirely.

Mountain bike advocacy—to form alliances; keep existing trails open; educate current and future riders and land managers and all users of the backcountry; and work on maintaining trails—is the hottest trend. The International Mountain Bicycling Association (IMBA) is spearheading efforts to educate cyclists and keep the trails open. Industry is also getting into the act, donating funds to IMBA's education efforts. IMBA's Share the Trails message is on T-shirts, signposts, water bottles, and industry ads. Now all mountain bikers are learning manners and how to make friends and alliances.

An exciting development is the Bureau of Land Management (BLM) involvement in the scene. The BLM manages 270 million acres of land and 65,000 miles of road, both paved and unpaved, in eleven western states. Its interest in working with mountain bikes has resulted in the creation of the 128-mile Kokopelli Trail, from Grand Junction, Colorado, to Moab, Utah. Bob Moore, BLM's Colorado State director, typifies BLM's commitment to mountain bikers, believing mountain bikes " . . . fit perfectly with BLM's concept of multiple use. It's another use that can be accommodated on BLM lands much like hiking or horseback riding or off-highway vehicle use where it's appropriate." So look to the future, off-road riders, the BLM has land in some prime territory. Watch BLM land in Alaska, Arizona, California, Colorado, Idaho, Montana, Nevada, New Mexico, Oregon, Utah, and Wyoming for future off-road trails.

So where does this lead us? To more and more options.

Cyclists can also pick from a plethora of bicycle clubs. Anytime more than two cyclists come together and decide on a name, they seem to automatically put out a newsletter. There are clubs in Taos, New Mexico; Greenville, South Carolina; Portland, Oregon; and El Cajon, California. There are clubs for road racers, mountain bike racers, road riders, gay and lesbian cyclists, mountain bike riders, single cyclists, triathletes, tandem enthusiasts, unicycle riders, recumbent cyclists, and so on. Clubs offer company, expert advice, and a supply of routes. After years of trial and error, they also know the best food stands. Can't see any reason not to join up—it's an easy bet forecasting their growth. NORBA (the National Off-Road Bicycle Association) had 6,000 members in 1989 and two years later, it's practically doubled to 11,000.

Clubs sponsor rides that often take on a life of their own. I survived the Greenville Spinners' Assault on Mt. Mitchell, a 100-mile challenge of a ride, that gains 5,000 feet of elevation in the last twenty-five miles. In 1982 I completed the assault, crawling the last five miles in my rock-bottom lowest gear. I had not eaten enough; the coolness was beginnning to fog the road, colliding with the hot air of the day just ending. My stomach was complaining; other riders could hear it, too. Speed was something turtles had; I was probably going just as fast as you could walk, and wondering if the damned mountaintop was retreating as I approached. A friend had finished hours before I did (he came in fifth out of a field of 220; nine years later some 1,800 get assaulted). I was annoyed at my strategy, or complete lack of it. Foolishly, I'd waited at the lunch stop for another buddy. I'd lingered forty-five minutes, long enough to cool down, cramp up, and lose momentum. And I hadn't eaten well, choosing greasy, fast food. Now I know better, and I've also got a huge smorgasbord of rides to attempt in every part of the country.

Some have the damndest names. Try any or all of the following: Fowl Crab Century (Delaware), Apple Cider Century (Michigan); Wolf Haven Century (Washington), Flying Wheels Challenge (Washington), Great Annual Peanut Rides (Virginia), Red Riding Hood (women only, put on by the men of the Bonneville Bicycle Touring Club in Utah), Dog Daze Century (Pennsylvania), No Baloney Century (Pennsylvania), The Morning Glory Ride (Ohio), Beast of the East (New Jersey), RAIN (Ride Across Indiana), Heart Cycle ATB (Colorado); Banana Classic (California); Women on the Roll (women's only, California); Hillier Than Thou Century (New Jersey); and Death Valley by Moonlight (California).

There are the human-powered vehicle (HPV) people. They're playful, often whimsically changing the bike's form and showcasing human power in its many guises. One of the purposes of the International Human Powered Vehicle Association (IHPVA), is to promote the design of human powered commuting vehicles. Marti Daily, president of the IHPVA, says "there are several designs that are enclosed and streetworthy." Perhaps an HPV will prove ideal for commuting, offering weather protection, cargo capacity, and consistent speeds of thirty mph.

Who could have predicted that good old Donald Trump would have the impact he has had on bicycle racing? His name graced the inaugural Tour de Trump,

123

since metamorphosed into the Tour Du Pont (better bicycling through chemicals). The Tour Du Pont stage race, one of the only ones of note in the U.S. racing calendar, should be around for at least another three years. Its presence heralds an increasing interest in racing, accelerated a bit with Greg LeMond's many wins, trumpeted on the front pages. Some races, such as Philadelphia's CoreStates, draw 200,000 spectators. Those large numbers just might affect coverage. Hopefully there will be more on the big networks, helping viewers understand the complexity, the teamwork, history, drama, and difficulty of racing. Perhaps with more mountain bike racing, there will be increased curiosity. There are some great off-road riders to watch: Jacquie Phelan (a.k.a. Alice B. Toeclips), John Tomac, Ruthie Matthes, Ned Overend, and Cindy Whitehead. Maybe TV coverage will creep down to John Marino, who has selflessly struggled for ten years to promote the 3,000-mile RAAM.

While most of us only fantasize about racing full-time, more folks seek a challenge like RAAM, perhaps taking one of the PAC Tours led by former RAAM winners Lon Haldeman and Susan Notorangelo. PAC Transcontinental is a mere 3,200 miles done in twenty-four days. That translates into 140 miles a day. Or head for the mountains, cycling PAC's Rockies, and do 100 to 120 miles a day.

Touring companies have evolved to offer any kind of on- or off-road adventure. They do less mileage than RAAM or PAC, that's for sure. Meander along the Russian River in northern California or tour Vermont's fall foliage (planning a necessary stop at Ben and Jerry's ice cream factory). Companies go to Tibet, Bali, Puget Sound, and every place in between. Cyclists choosing to direct their own path have access to maps designed by Bikecentennial, by and for cyclists. Charities have realized the earning and consciousness-raising potential of bike-a-thons. Hundreds of them happen all over the country each season.

As the Wright brothers knew, it all begins with a set of wheels. However, I'd love to see the Wright brothers, those guys who moved from an Ohio bicycle shop to designing planes, try and get a boxed bicycle on a domestic flight. Ha!

While the sky may practically be the limit, flying through it via airplane with a checked bike is a drag. Don't ask me why golf clubs, skis, huge boxes, and unwieldy suitcases the size of pianos fly for free and bikes do not. Don't ask me why you as a cyclist flying with a well-packed bicycle have the privilege of paying twenty-five to fifty dollars for taking your bike in one direction and simultaneously signing away any right to claim damages. Someone told me the airlines have never heard anyone complain about this, so the practice persists. Humbug! I've certainly let a few words fly. Politely, of course. And I have successfully collected from Braniff when it made pasta salad out of my box and bike. But, hey, fly internationally and you enter another realm. They don't make it tough for you to take a bicycle. I'd like to see our domestic carriers do the same. Will it happen? Only if we make it so.

Never underestimate the power of activists. Passion, letters, nonprofit organizations, and groups of people

nudging elected officials can get things happening. Rails-to-Trails is a case in point. When started in 1986, Rails-to-Trails estimated sixty to eighty trails existed, approximately 750 miles. As of 1991, there were nearly 5,000 miles of converted rail-trails, offering cyclists, equestrians, hikers, skiers, runners, and walkers a ribbon of green. Rails-to-Trails continues to grow and can see an inner connected network of greenways and rail-trails connecting all cities, counties, and communities from coast to coast. What a legacy this would be for anyone seeking a corridor of calming green, a perimeter of nature.

Bikecentennial offers the promise of more routes for the future, too. Its National Bicycle Trails Network is wrapping up its mapping of long-distance routes and is now going regional. With the completion of the Southern California-to-Florida route in 1992, some 19,000 miles will be detailed in their map packages. Next focus will be creating tie-ins for existing routes. Doing a Bikecentennial route, or any swath across the United States, is a rite of passage for many. In 1976, the year of America's bicentennial, over 4,000 cyclists went to look for America following Bikecentennial's newly mapped TransAmerica Bicycle Trail. Half went the entire 4,500 miles.

Check out other programs to set aside green space for shared recreational use. In 1998, California's Bay Area will have a 400-mile trail system for hikers, equestrians, and mountain bicyclists. The Bay Area Ridge Trail will connect over seventy-five parks; currently 120 miles are completed.

Bicycling will continue to take us down all sorts of roads and off the beaten track, influencing and changing lives. "Entertainment Tonight" co-anchor, commentator for CBS Sports, and musician John Tesh believes "the sport of cycling changed my life." His first experience with the Tour de France showed him a pageantry and level of athletic competition that he couldn't believe. Now, "Everything I do is based on the passion I learned from the Tour de France." Others, such as Representatives Jim McDermott and Joseph Kennedy, make a place for cycling in their daily lives. Representative McDermott's fondest dream is "to make it possible for people to safely bicycle to work."

So what does all this mean? With any luck, more people will be enticed to bicycling as a sport and way of life. Some will become involved with advocacy and work the front lines to catalyze needed change. Others will motivate friends, turning them into cycling companions. There is and will be much to plan for.

On my bicycle, I am a pilgrim, a happy supplicant. The world is right before me, rich in all its offerings, and every neighborhood I pass through is much more than a quick point on a map. The bike's openness and unobtrusiveness makes it accessible. Who could be wary of a bicycle? I bypass nothing, even if I quicken my pace. It's a day in which anything that happens is sufficient. The play of light, a dog approaching, barking subserviently, hindquarters a complete wag and brown eyes eager. Here the senses are given gifts. Here there is weather to be dealt with, not hurried through in a metal-and-glass enclosure, to be avoided like the plague. If we take such care to always avoid wetness and wind, what else will we miss? How much of our senses will dull, collapse in on themselves like dehydrated plants?

I look forward to the seasons, cycling way below snow geese on the Central Flyway, from Hudson Bay, in Canada, to Mexico. I look to the bicycle to provide a sense of place and belonging. To browse sidestreets, discovering bakeries, city parks, and places where people sit, watching the day unfold. Sometimes, I reflect on *Ecotopia*, an Ernest Callenbach classic in the political/sci-fi category. It proposes a time when several states secede from the nation to form an environmentally oriented society. In this utopia, bikes are left willy-nilly for people to pick up and ride anywhere. There are small towns and a feeling of family and community.

Gary Fisher, bike designer and builder, says of the bicycle, "It's a true friend of the environment." And it truly is. By extension, it's a friend to all, of all ages and abilities.

Now and again, the world closes in on me like a stultifying, small shell, and my thoughts drift back to places I've gone long distance touring. Other territories and the wonderful plane of motion—the country of all travelers—return clearly. Of course, remembrance is a distant cousin to experience, but finally if all the textures, smells and sounds come crowding in, I'm on a trip again, out on the proverbial road.

I stand before Lake Victoria in Australia. The moon is almost full, its light brilliant like an eye, revealing my thoughts, my fears. It's three A.M., on the third or fourth day of a three-week bicycle tour from Melbourne to Sydney. Tents flutter in a breeze, the lake gleams, an expanse of black mirror. All around me are sleep sounds. There's a comforting hum, the innocence of slumber. I can see the shape of bodies through tentcloth, sprawled like gentle mountain ranges.

As I walk around the campsite, carefully skirting the strewn bicycles and equipment from 2,200 cyclists on this trip celebrating Australia's bicentennial, I am the only person alive. The others are shadows, sleeping quietly in the night. The foreignness, yet familiarity of Australia, is like a remarkable license to be whatever I wish.

From behind a fence, I can hear the stirrings of kangaroos, sure in their sanctuary. What wondrous beasts they are: their strong hindquarters remind me of our quad muscles, strengthened by bicycling and now more powerful over the hills. I'm riveted by the 'roos' huge eyes, and by the whole notion of marsupials and pouches. Few things seem as funny or as touching as a joey (a baby kangaroo) zipping in so quickly that his feet poke out like nervous sticks.

And wombats. I love that word: thick, furry beasts so unlike anything in the States. Unfortunately, I've never spied one along the road, although I search the gum trees as we go by. I alternate scouring the ground with peering upward into the trees for koalas. Between Dandenong and Warragul, Rosedale and Orbost, I keep an eye out for animals I will see only here.

This is Oz, the land of Dreamtime, murmurs of thousands of years, older inhabitants and their way of being. Aboriginal people and their song created this world, naming the animals, the spirits. By bicycle, I feel able to claim a connection. Moving between cities and towns on two wheels, breathing the air across wide valleys, feeling the wind between its travels, attaches me to this land. This is my walkabout. In the quiet of others' sleep, I practice my "G'day, Mate."

Australia. There's beer—served in middies, schooners or pots—new mates, meat pies, and the pull of a continent a whole day's flight away. So strange riding on the left side of the road. I constantly have to thwart my desire to pull right.

I don't remember having that problem in Ireland. But that minor bicycle excursion was decades ago. My memory has selected an image of me on a 40-pound clunk of a 3-speed rental bike somewhere near Dingle, my satchel stuffed with hearty brown bread. Ireland, where I learned to love warm Guinness beer and the toothy smiles I encountered. Early November rain and amazing rainbows. So unlike other rainbows that I kept hoping that yes, indeed, there'd be something, somewhere near the end. Instead I found battered stones shaped into castles and fences, the history of hard work. Ireland, where I remembered I could ride any bicycle, regardless of its condition.

Every trip allows me to create my own chronicle and to be totally immersed in the moment. On the cool, damp road to Canberra, Australia's capital, I yearn for chocolate, cappucino, or anything hot. Susan and I tell stories. The small of my back, the space where my shirt rides up and my shorts ride down, aches from the damp. To my left, a plain seemingly as wide as all Montana, a fringe of ever-present gum trees. The water in the road runs in rivulets. Happy frogs sing in fresh puddles. The air flows through every pore of my lungs, cleaning them out and waking me up.

"What I'd give for a hot, hot shower," Susan muses.

"Hmm, me too," I respond. Okay, life now consists of food fantasies, gentle twinges, and the constant readiness to see a kangaroo, kookaburra or wombat. Such a freedom in simplicity. If we ever lived in another life, it seems long gone. A jeep with a 'roo bar passes us on the left. It's a big, box-like vehicle, one that jaunts across the outback, bouncing over the hard roads. I see the driver's hand raised in greeting, can almost hear the wonderfully casual, only in Australia, "G'day."

Try as I might over the miles and days of this tour, I can't consistently get that hello just right. Besides, I'm focused on hot stuff now: coffee, tea, soup. Susan and I are plotting a total, shoes off enjoyment of the first café we can attack. If there's a world beyond the space in which I ride, it doesn't exist for me. This is a bountiful harvest for my future; a total immersion into the where of a place, bathing in the physical world.

The vast open spaces approaching Canberra, some populated by cattle, don't seem to change much. We ride side by side, sometimes one of us pulling ahead to draft. From under her helmet, Susan's blond hair stands out against the muted greens, grays and blue-greens of this unseasonably cool summer. When you're cold, wind-blown and slightly grumpy, bicycle miles can seem unusually long. Talking makes the inches move quicker. Ahead, the helmets of other cyclists bob like colored corks above the endless Australian plains.

There are clusters of homes and other hints that a metropolis is nearby. Canberra, a new city designed by

American architect Walter Burley Griffin, is so close I can almost smell what I've been fancying. Bus stops, really cozy little shelters, line the route. They're painted with the artwork of masters. One resting cyclist looks like he's in front of a Matisse, its bright colors blooming behind him.

Down the road Susan and I skip. We fly the ten or so miles from the edge of the city to near its center. Midblock and straight ahead, a tiny café and there's no line! The two of us park the bikes, practically leaping at scones. Feet up on chairs, lingering over dregs of round two of hot chocolate, we survey our world. It is a grand one.

There are few excuses for not cycling. You can bicycle at almost any time, whether the temperature is cold or warm, and at any age.

You can cycle in a downpour, although you may choose to sit it out in a barn. (If there's thunder and lightning, forget huddling under a tree.) Hot weather doesn't need to hold you back, either. Drink plenty of water, wear cool, light-colored clothes, and try a damp bandanna around your neck. I've pedaled down Baja's Highway One feeling, at times, like a batch of frijoles on a skillet. But I've lacquered myself with sunscreen, flooded the kidneys, and thought oasislike thoughts; of ice cream with small arctic crystals; an isolated lake, its water breathtakingly frigid; white clothes, cool to the touch, and a cold beer in a chilled glass. Actually, I find the air feels cooler when I bicycle than when I stop. Of course, pacing is important; the idea is to work with the weather, not go for heat exhaustion.

Cold temperatures present other challenges, but here, too, not many excuses will work. You can cycle till icicles threaten to become a permanent fixture on your face. Ice on roads or trails is a definite no for me, although I know of others who can stay upright on it. Guess they're working on entering the 200-mile Iditabike in Alaska. Cold is no problem, though; I've pushed the pedals when it's been fifteen degrees Fahrenheit and windy. A Windbreaker, hood, scarf, gloves under mittens, two pair of socks, and wool on both my upper and lower torso has stood me well. I've arrived exhilarated, with red cheeks, a tremendous appetite for hot chocolate, and a slightly wind-bitten sense of accomplishment.

When the temperature is below freezing, conditions remain dry, and comfort depends on the balance between how much clothing you wear, and your riding pace. Dress in layers of clothes that can easily be added or subtracted, rather than a single, bulky garment. Tip: If you are comfortable at the start of a ride, you are too warmly dressed.

Cold weather and even snow are fun, but freezing rain turns me into a marshmallow and can be dangerous. The combination of wet, cold, and wind have a devastatingly chilling effect, and can cause hypothermia. Always be careful in such conditions, especially when coasting downhill. If you become too cold, do not persist in riding until too late; stop the bike to eliminate wind chill, cover up as much as possible, and move around to warm yourself up. Another tip: On descents, pedal backward to keep the blood moving in your legs.

You can bicycle until you die. And you can start when you're just a wee tyke, just old enough for your neck muscles to safely support the weight of a helmet. In between, well, there's the world . . . and then some. As near as I can figure, I've put in 70,000 miles on my road and mountain bikes, plus a couple of hundred on a tandem, and a few pitiful ones on a too-large recumbent. Almost enough to go around the earth at the equator three times. Once around is a mere 24,902 miles, so I plan on pedaling as long as I can keep air in my tires and past when they invent an airless tube for the masses. Then I'll contemplate joining the human-powered-vehicle folks and asking if they'd like a slow but seasoned test pilot for the Gossamer or whatever pedal-powered flight machine they're currently fiddling with.

As demographers are so fond of incessantly pointing out, the population is aging. And the number of older people cycling is increasing, naturally.

There are more cyclists racing in the Masters category, thirty and over. The U.S. National Senior Olympics, begun in 1987, has competitions every two years. I've been shamed one too many times to ever believe gray hair means slower on the spin. Being passed by people over the age of sixty assures me I can bicycle for many, many decades and that I've got a chance, maybe, to catch up with them. After all, how can you be over the hill if you keep pedaling over them again and again?

There's Botto, a gentleman of seventy, spinning down Baja with me. We were two out of thirty-five cyclists surviving Bob Wagner's yearly "Deathmarch Down Baja." An 1,100-mile rugged challenge of a trip with no sag and occasionally primitive camping (translation: cactus and view), where you carried your own equipment plus

135

a gallon of water and some food. (A gallon of liquid weighs approximately eight pounds; I added to that emergency supply by stashing a small container of chunky peanut butter and some taco shells. The shells were always soggy and in pieces. Tasty.)

Botto's trim figure was a flag on the desert's horizon. He was usually ahead of me, even on the 140-mile day. And he rarely seemed to be breaking a sweat. But at seventy, he was young. Then lest you think Botto an anomaly, there was Glenn Ingram, a King Arthur legend on RAGBRAI, who completed six of those 500-mile cross-state tours. On a doctor's advice, Glenn gave up running in his seventies and switched to bicycling. Every year on RAGBRAI, he wore a specially composed T-shirt. The first year I spotted him we had both discovered warm cinnamon breakfast rolls and his message, I'm 79 and Doing Fine, made me chuckle for at least three miles. Then there was Just turned 80 and Still with the Same Sweet Lady. Another year brought Just Take Care of Your Body, You Only Have One. Not too long ago, he succumbed to brain cancer, having credited cycling with enriching and extending his life. Jane Schnell, a youngster in her sixties, typifies a lot of similar people who take to the road after retirement. She's pedaled at least 15,000 miles on her bicycle, returning home to write about it in her book *Changing Gears*.

Many RAAM or Race Across AMerica contestants are, in my mother's enduring words, "no spring chickens," but successfully complete one of the toughest ultramarathon cycling challenges around. While the course varies from year to year, participants can count on 3,000

or so hilly, windy, unpredictable hot miles. There's Susan Notorangelo, mother of two, and Casey Patterson, mother of three, who won the women's RAAM on separate occasions. When she was forty-three years old, Casey took the 1987 RAAM, crossing the finish line in Washington, D.C., 11 days, 21 hours, and 15 minutes and 3,127 miles after she began at Golden Gate Bridge. Hard to believe she had started cycling only in 1981, when her son Kye Sharp built her a mountain bike. Casey claims that "changed the course of my life. It got me into bicycling at thirty-seven." If you think you're too old to start, think again. Casey had never raced until she was thirty-eight years old, when she won her first, a mountain bike race in Malibu, California.

I led a tour for Open Road, now folded into Bicycle Vermont, which had a sixtyish librarian who hadn't been on a bicycle in five years. While I certainly wouldn't recommend going on a tour if you haven't ridden recently (risky business), she did fine. Practically anyone in decent shape with a comfortable bicycle can crank out at least five miles.

Sometimes, long after your ankles and knees have taken a pounding from running, there's bicycling. It's easier on the joints, especially if instead of pushing the cranks slowly and hard, you spin them rapidly and lightly. There isn't the impact on your legs that running entails. And if you're a bit tired, you can always ease your pace.

Cycling is great exercise. Dr. Gabe Mirkin, author of six books on sports medicine, including, *The Sports Medicine Book*, says that "all the measures of aging that we have are measures of fitness." So when we look at an individual's physical fitness we view VO_2 (oxygen uptake)

Older Cyclists

Bicycle Adventure Club, 3904 Groton St., San Diego, CA 92110, tel.: 619/226-2175.

Keep on Pedaling: The Complete Guide to Adult Bicycling, *by Norman D. Ford (The Countrymen Press: Woodstock, VT)*

U.S. National Senior Sports Organization, 14323 S. Outer Forty Rd., Ste. N300, Chesterfield, MO 63017, tel.: 314/878-4900.

International Bicycle Tours, 7 Champlin Square, P.O. Box 754, Essex, CT 06426, tel.: 203/767-7005.

Record Challenge Time Trial, P.O. Box 40235, Albuquerque, NM 87198, tel.: 505/884-1880.

maximum, recovering pulse rates, blood pressure, and cholesterol level. It comes as no surprise that when doctors study older people who exercise into later life, many are physically younger. Dr. Mirkin emphasizes that "the data is strong that calorie and fat restriction staves off aging and that people who exercise are generally healthy." And bicycling, says Dr. Mirkin, "is the safest exercise around, if you don't fall. It doesn't tear up muscles and it's easier on joints."

Physical disabilities can often be surmounted. If your vision doesn't permit you to cycle solo, you can contribute your legs to a tandem team. If your balance isn't what it once was, there is a feast of builders and designers who will work with you. The Counterpoint tandem, which allows the front person to either pedal or not, helps people with vision or limb loss. Hand-pedaled bikes also aid those who've lost a limb, although many still use the traditional diamond-frame bicycle. Independence and mobility can be yours at practically any age due to the wonderful range of options.

Under the care of a doctor, pregnant women find cycling an exercise they can do well into their pregancy. Fifteen years ago my friend Casey rode until her sixth month. Another friend, Donna, from Ohio, just completed a seventy-mile ride in her eighth month.

I initally met Donna and her daughter Sara in Australia, cycling the 700 miles from Melbourne to Sydney. Sara, age five, had first started in a child-mounted carrier. As she got bigger, her mother added a trailer. The low center of gravity and vaster quantity of toys Sara could smuggle aboard appealed to both. When I encountered

them, Sara, age five, was happily soaking up the attention most of the other 2,300 members of the ride were giving her. All Donna's 106 pounds were successfuly pulling 70 pounds of trailer, child, and supplies. Both were having a blast. Now Donna has a tandem; Sara, at age eight, is the stoker and has done eight 100-mile centuries in 1991 (she wants to do as many centuries as she is old). Donna, remarried and six months pregnant, just completed an easy century. For Donna, it's simple: "My knees just go out to the sides, and I raise my handlebars a bit." She now rides a single bike and says, "It feels good cycling. It stretches out my back and it's non-weightbearing, so my legs aren't developing varicose veins." She assures me she won't pedal to the hospital while in labor.

Cycling is incredibly democratic. What has amazed and heartened me is the range of people who flock to it. On RAGBRAI, two nine-year-old boys, twins outfitted in matching black shorts and rainbow suspenders, kept pace with most cyclists and rode the entire 500 miles. I'd periodically see their Bell-helmeted heads bobbing in the distance. They were having fun, but they were determined. Then there's the two-fisted handful of cyclists in their seventies that I've met on long-distance tours. One kept up a blistering pace in Australia as we celebrated Australia's Bicentennial. At seventy-six, he was smooth and disarmingly faster than many cyclists—of any age.

Mountain biking is also within anyone's reach. Older and younger cyclists are cycling on gentle dirt trails, fire trails, and on hard-packed routes, such as the 150-mile Chesapeake & Ohio Trail from Washington, D.C., to Cumberland, Maryland. My friend Linda and I took our mountain bikes and snacks down this trail. Far away from the city and people, we found a field for a quick nap in the late-fall afternoon, surrounded by river noise and wind, the last of the crickets, and the crackle of twigs. Sprawled on grass and surrounded by quiet, we rested, having tested our bikes' ability to handle ruts, mud, and gravel.

Other times, we take our dirt bikes out of the country—for example, to Belize in Central America. There, on a ride organized by the Touring Exchange, another cyclist and I went down a long cut, exploring a thickly graveled road that led to a Mennonite community. A bit off the beaten track and thirsty, we stopped alongside two towheaded children carrying a basket of eggs. The common denominator was the bicycle; we were at eye level. Although shy, the brother and sister warmed to us, directing us to their home, where their mother plied us with pitchers of cool water. We had similar experiences throughout the rest of the ride. The bicycle is a communal creature. Open on all sides, it enables its rider to wave to a neighbor, stop for a moment and be there.

When I'm older I want to cycle in Idaho on the Sawtooth Mountains, the youngest mountain range in the United States. I want to learn the stars, so that when I'm cycling in the summer and the Summer Triangle or the Great Square of Pegasus appears, I have words and another way to locate myself. When I bicycle, I try and leave the clock behind. Find other means of time and fix myself on simpler persuasions: the oncoming dusk, the need for food, or encroaching tiredness and the welcome presence of friends.

Sometimes I believe the best doctor to be my bicycle.

Stress, depression, tension, and discomfort usually vanish after a few miles. Others have felt this way, too. In his 1895 book, *Pleasure-Cycling*, Henry Clyde quotes a woman who discovered that "the bicycle has been the greatest of blessings to my husband. He has always seemed fairly well, but always nervous, and at times afflicted with the worst attacks of 'the blues.' These never visit him now in wheeling season, and I shall welcome for his sake the opening spring and settled roads."

Riding on a silk road, a fluid trail, the sound of the wheels smooth as the golden notes of a saxophone flowing over the horizon. Riding effortlessly at dusk, floating over the place where earth and sky meet. The spokes are a clarinet, thin and reedy. My tool bag, bells: extra nuts and bolts, wrenches, and change clinking together. Then there's the cacophony of inner music, my constant hum of delight occasionally punctuated by philosophical questions—sort of like the French horn in Prokofiev's *Peter and the Wolf*— questions of destination and ways of going. Or there's the banter with others about necessary connections to make, talk about the next food stop, the feel of the weather.

A fall ride near Round Hill, Virginia, with friend Debra. It's hilly, we are a bit out of shape, but the air is blue and cool, the leaves bright and golden. Suddenly the skies open up, cold and rain. The miles go by ever so slowly; we fill them with complaints and fantasies. (Never underestimate the cathartic power of bitching.) I'm daydreaming tomato soup, grilled-cheese sandwiches, and warmth. Down a steep hill, across a busy road, and there, tucked away in a gas station, is a homey resturant. Wet but welcomed, Debra and I find, yes, the food we've been dreaming of. Warmth spreads from the stomach out. The rain moves off elsewhere. Sometimes magic means simple wishes coming true.

Boredom might be a problem at some point. Even cycling can feel tiresome now and again. Try variety. Tired of road biking? Try mountain biking. Weary of mountain biking? Borrow a friend's tandem. Or take a course in botany and take your new knowledge of flora on the road with you. Sign up for a bike-repair course, a class in mountain biking. Try Rollerblading or cross-country skiing. Get into weight lifting. Help your local advocacy group improve trails or bridge access. Work to elect officials who take into account alternative transportation. Design a route and bring your friends.

Sometimes sharing your life sport with others reinvigorates you, reminding you how you felt about bicycling in the beginning. I'm fond of the Bicycle Action Project, Kids on Bikes, and other programs that help inner-city youths. Organize a bike rodeo. Or plan an adventure. Feeling every club ride is a double déjà vu? Go for an across-the-country, once-in-a-lifetime trek. Get involved in racing. Check out the local velodrome or work to build one. Help others learn to bicycle. If you don't already, commute to work. See how many routes you can design to get to the same place. Volunteer as a timekeeper for RAAM or spend two weeks as a volunteer for the Tour Du Pont. Plan a vacation around the yearly summer Human Powered Vehicle Championships. Curl up when it's really cold with a book on bicycle adventurers.

Just think, you might turn into Dan Buettner. Dan is entered twice in the *Guinness Book of Records*, first for

Bicycle Outreach

Looking to share your love of cycling or help others discover it? The following groups work with at-risk youth and can offer pointers and information.

Trips for Kids, 138 Sunnyside, Mill Valley, CA 94941.

Bicycle Action Project, 948 N. Alabama, Indianapolis, IN 46202, tel.: 317/631-1326.

Pedal Power Camp, 4-H Youth Development, 340 Coffey Hall, University of Minnesota, St. Paul, MN 55108, tel.: 612/625-9719.

cycling the length of the Americas, from Alaska to Argentina, second for the Soviet Trek, a 12,888-mile tour on which Dan believes he "learned more on 308 days of bicycling than in eighteen years of education." Dan has made cycling a career because it ". . . enrich(es) the body, mind and spirit in a way no other vocation can. The routine of bicycling 100 miles per day keeps the body in supreme physical shape. . . . You travel slowly enough to actually get a feel for what it's like to live in the countries through which you're passing. And when you are old and looking back, you'll take solace in knowing that life didn't pass you by; your wheel kept pace right along side."

This is what we have access to every day, an expedition, an adventure. As bicyclists we are alchemists, spinning the long, thin drudge of days into a ribbon on the road. Down this path we glide, and behind us is the day, falling away. Ahead is what we notice. Even on those bad, off-key days, when rain dribbles down our necks, followed by a flat tire or unpleasant encounter, there's a sense of coping, of outwitting Rumplestilskin. How great it feels to be in control, even if we cannot (nor would we want to, I suspect) control everything around us. The heavens may storm, the sky may darken like a bruise, and the sun may disappear, seemingly forever. Hail may litter the road, but we can put foot to pedal and move forward. We can relocate and take whatever companions we choose—friends, thoughts, or dreams. We can spin gold from straw. And we can come to the same journey and share words, food, and the love of what is just over the hill, around the corner, the beginning of a horizon that we create.

GENERAL CYCLING RESOURCES

Organizations

American Bicycle Association (ABA), P.O. Box 714, Chandler, AZ 85244, tel.: 602/961-1903. For big and little kids—organizes BMX races.

Bay Area Ridge Trail Council, 116 New Montgomery, Ste. 640, San Francisco, CA 94105, tel.: 415/543-4291. Working to establish a 400-mile trail system in California's Bay Area.

Bicycle Federation of America, 1818 R St. NW, Washington, D.C. 20009, tel.: 202/332-6986. Promotes all aspects of bicycling, publishes *Pro Bike News*, and conducts research on bike-trail planning and safety.

Bicycle Helmet Safety Institute, 4611 Seventh St., South Arlington, VA 22204, tel.: 703/486-0100. Document center on all aspects of bicycle helmets.

The Bicycle Network, P.O. Box 8194, Philadelphia, PA 19101. Publishes cycling calendar and *The Network News*, a bicycle clipping service.

Bikecentennial, P.O. Box 8308, Missoula, MT 59807, tel.: 406/721-1776. Largest non-profit recreational cycling organization. Has 28,000 members. Publishes *The Cyclist's Yellow Pages*.

Campaign for New Transportation Priorities, 900 Second St. NE, Ste. 308, Washington, D.C. 20002, tel.: 202/408-8362. Coalition of environmental, labor, and consumer organizations.

Canadian Cycling Association, 1600 James Naismith Dr., Gloucester, Ontario K1B 5N4, Canada, tel.: 613/748-5629.

Information on touring and maps.

Classic Bicycle and Whizzer Club of America, 35769 Simon Fraser, MI 48026, tel.: 313/791-5594. For old bicycle enthusiasts.

Family Cycling Club FCC R.R. 8, Box 319E, Glenwood Dr., Bridgeton, NJ 08302, tel.: 609/451-5104. Encourages family cycling.

Human Powered Transit Association, P.O. Box 1552, Reseda, CA 91337, tel.: 818/988-7728. Promotes bicycle commuting.

Institute for Transportation and Development Policy (ITDP), 1787 Columbia Rd. NW, Washington, D.C. 20009, tel.: 202/387-1434. Non-profit organization that promotes sustainable, non-motorized transportation systems. Umbrella organization for Mobility Haiti.

International Human Powered Vehicle Association, P.O. Box 51255, Indianapolis, IN 46251. Promotes human-powered vehicles of all kinds. Produces the yearly Human Powered Vehicle Championships.

International Mountain Bicycling Association, P.O. Box 412043, Los Angeles, CA 90041, tel.: 818/792-8830. Promotes open trails and fireroads through responsible bicycling. Works to educate land managers, mountain bicyclists, and the public.

International Randonneurs, 7272 N. Salina St., Syracuse, NY 13224. Sponsors qualifying rides throughout the United States for the 750-mile Paris-Brest-Paris marathon ride.

League of American Wheelmen (L.A.W.), 190 W. Ostend

St., Ste. 120, Baltimore, MD 21230, tel.: 301/539-3399. National organization of bicyclists. Has 21,000 members. Publishes *Bicycle USA*.

National Bicycle Center, P.O. Box 3401, Redmond, WA 98073, tel.: 206/869-5804. Establishing an international sporting facility. Designs programs.

National Bicycle League, 211 Bradenton Ave., Ste. 100, Dublin, OH 43017, tel.: 614/766-1625. Sanctioning organization for BMX and freestyle racing.

National Bike Registry, 1832 Tribute Rd., Sacramento, CA 95815, tel.: 800/848-BIKE. For $5 a year, registers bike. Helps with recovery.

National Off-Road Bicycling Association (NORBA), 1750 E. Boulder St., Colorado Springs, CO 80909, tel.: 719/578-4717. Oversees off-road racing in the United States.

Pacelines, 43 Upton St., Boston, MA 02118. Cycling network for gay and lesbian cyclists and their friends.

Perimeter Bicycle Association, 630 N. Craycroft, Ste. 127, Tucson, AZ 85711, tel.: 602/745-2033. Sponsors the annual El Tour de Tucson and encourages perimeter bicycling events.

Rails-to-Trails Conservancy, 1400 Sixteenth St. NW, Ste. 300, Washington, D.C. 20036, tel.: 202/797-5400. A nonprofit organization dedicated to converting abandoned railroad rights-of-way into multipurpose trails.

Recumbent Bicycle Club of America, 427-3 Amherst St., Ste. 305, Nashua, NH 03063. For recumbent cyclists.

The Tandem Club of America, 2220 Vaness Dr., Birmingham, AL 35242. Encourages tandem cyclists and sponsors regional rallies.

Transportation Alternatives, 494 Broadway, New York, NY 10012, tel.: 212/941-4600. Devoted to improving bicycle access.

Ultra Marathon Cycling Association, 2761 North Marengo Ave., Altadena, CA 91001, tel.: 818/794-3119. Produces the yearly RAAM (Race Across AMerica), publishes newsletter, and supports long-distance bicycling events.

U.S. Cycling Federation, 1750 E. Boulder St., Colorado Springs, CO 80909, tel.: 719/578-4581. Directs amateur racing in the United States.

United States Professional Cycling Federation, Rt. 1, Box 1650, New Tripoli, PA 18066, tel.: 215/298-3262. Governs professional cycling in the United States.

The Wheelmen, 1708 School House Ln., Ambler, PA 19002. Nationwide club interested in old bicycles. Organizes regional and national meets.

Worldwatch Institute, 1776 Massachusetts Ave. NW, Washington, D.C. 20036, tel.: 202/452-1999. Non-profit organization that publishes *The State of the World* and other books of worldwide environmental concern.

Women's Organizations

Women's Cycling Coalition, P.O. Box 281, Louisville, CO 80027, tel.: 303/666-0500.

Women's Cycling Network, P.O. Box 73, Harvard, IL 60033. Promotes women's participation in bicycling. Publishes newsletter.

WOMBATS (Women's Mountain Bike and Tea Society), P.O. Box 757, Fairfax, CA 94930. Mountain bike group for women with sense of humor. Publishes newsletter.

Women's Sports Foundation, 342 Madison Ave., Ste. 728, New York, NY 10173, tel.: 212/972-9170. Encourages all women's athletic endeavors.

Women-Only Rides

Cinderella Classic Valley Spokesmens Touring Club, P.O. Box 2630, Dublin, CA 94568, tel.: 510/828-5299. A sixty-mile ride the last Saturday in March.

Heartland Bicycle Tours, One Orchard Circle, Washington, IA 52353, tel.: 800/798-2859. WOW (Women On Wheels) tour.

Ore-Ida Women's Challenge, P.O. Box 10, Boise, ID 83707, tel.: 800/782-7180, 208/345-RACE. A 580-mile, women-only race held in Boise, Idaho. Typically eleven days long.

Red Riding Hood Bonneville Bicycle Touring Club, 3247 Bon View Dr., Salt Lake City, UT 84109, tel.: 801/278-9386. Mid-June ride, the Sunday before Father's Day.

Snow White 60 Bikes Plus, 1313 N. Rand Rd., Arlington Heights, IL 60004, tel.: 708/398-1650. Mid-June ride. "Men needed to work."

Touring Exchange, Box 265, Port Townsend, WA 98368, tel.: 206/385-0667. Can offer women-only tours to Baja, Costa Rica, and elsewhere.

Tour of the European Community Féminin (replacement for the Tour De France Féminin). Bicycling opportunities for women only.

Un Tour Des Femmes McLean County Wheelers, 100 N. Linden St., Normal, IL 61761. June ride in Illinois.

Women on Wheels, P.O. Box 13001, Lansing, MI 48901. June ride in Michigan.

Womentrek, 1411 E. Olive Way, Box 20643, Seattle, WA 98102, tel.: 206/325-4772.

Woodswomen, 25 W. Diamon Lake Rd., Minneapolis, MN 55419, tel.: 612/822-3809.

Books, Magazines, and Newsletters

Bicycling Magazine's Cycling for Women, Rodale Press, Emmaus, PA.

Miles From Nowhere, by Barbara Savage, The Mountaineers, Seattle, WA: 1983. A classic around-the-world story. Not to be missed.

Outdoor Woman, P.O. Box 834, Nyack, NY 10960, tel.: 914/358-1257. Ten times a year for women interested in bicycling and other sports.

The Woman Cyclist, by Elaine Mariolle and Michael Shermer, Contemporary Books, Chicago, IL: 1989. I prize this book for its portrait of the variety of cyclists out there. Not for women only.

A Woman's Guide to Cycling, by Susan Weaver, Ten Speed Press, Berkeley, CA: 1991. Comprehensive guide, encouraging, and fun to read.

Women's Sports and Fitness, 1919 14th St., Ste. 421, Boulder, CO 80302, tel.: 303/440-5111.

Two Wheels and A Taxi, by Virginia Urrutia, The Mountaineers Books, Seattle, WA: 1989. A grandmother cycles through the Andes.

Museums

Traveling? Consider the following museums, which have a bicycle component.

Carillon Park, 2001 S. Patterson Blvd., Dayton, OH, tel.: 513/293-2841. Offers a reproduction of the Wright Cycle Shop.

The Franklin Institute Science Museum and Planetarium, 20th and Ben Franklin Pkwy., Philadelphia, PA 19103, tel.: 215/448-1200. Go to Philadelphia for the Liberty Bell and this grand museum.

Henry Ford Museum, 20900 Oakwood Blvd., Dearborn, MI 48121, tel.: 313/271-1620. Much more than the auto resides here.

Mountain Bike Hall of Fame and Museum, P.O. Box 1961, Crested Butte, CO 81224, tel.: 303/349-7280. Struggling, small, and immensely interesting.

Museum of Science and Industry, 57th St. and Lakeshore Dr., Chicago, IL 60637, tel.: 312/684-1414.

New York Museum of Transportation, Box 136, West Henrietta, NY 14586, tel.: 716/533-1113.

Smithsonian's National Museum of American History, 14th and Constitution Ave. NW, Washington, D.C. 20560, tel.: 202/357-1300. In the Road Transportation Hall, there are seventeen bicycles on exhibit, dating from 1819 to 1989.

Schwinn History Center, tel.: 312/454-7471. Here's another build-it-and-they-will-come vision. Currently without a permanent, open-to-the-public home, the Schwinn History Center can receive calls. When it is open, it will be one of the best in the world.

Wheelsmith, Inc., 225 Hamilton Ave., Palo Alto, CA 94301, tel.: 415/324-0510. A store, workshop, and museum.

Museums Outside the United States

Canberra Bicycle Museum, 2 Badham St., Dickson, ACT Australia, tel.: 062 48 0999. This is located in a pub and features all sorts of exotic memorabilia.

Denmark's Cykel Museum, Borgergade 10, DK-9620 Aalestrup, Denmark, tel.: 1 45 9864 1960. A great museum in a country where 30 percent of all trips are by bicycle.

Deutsches Zweirad-Museum, Urbanstrasse 11, 7107, Neckarsulum, Germany, tel.: 07132 35271. Famous museum of only bicycles.

London Science Museum, Exhibition Rd., South Kensington, London SW7 2OD, tel.: 71 938 8000.

Museum of Sport and Bicycling, 118 Avenue President Kennedy, 75775 Paris, CEDEX 16, France. I haven't gone here yet but would love to.

Tokyo Bicycle Cultural Center, Jitenshakaikan #3, Bldg. 1-9-3, Akasaka, Minato-ku, Tokyo 107, Japan.

Velorama Waackade 107, 65 11 XR Nijmegen, Netherlands, tel.: 080 225 851. Cyclists in the know make a stop here. □

BIBLIOGRAPHY

Magazines and Newsletters

Antique/Classic Bicycle News, P.O. Box 1049, Ann Arbor, MI 48106.

Bicycle Forum, P.O. Box 8308, Missoula, MT 59807, tel.: 406/721-1776.

Bicycle Guide, 711 Boylston St., Boston, MA 02116, tel.: 617/236-1885.

Bicycle USA, League of American Wheelmen, 190 W. Ostend St., Ste. 120, Baltimore, MD 21230, tel.: 301/539-3399.

Bicycling, Rodale Press, Inc., 33 E. Minor St., Emmaus, PA 18098, tel.: 215/967-5171.

Bike Events, Bike Events, Ltd., P.O. Box 75, Bath BA1 1BX, Avon, England.

BikeReport, Bikecentennial, P.O. Box 8308, Missoula, MT 59807, tel.: 406/721-1776.

Cycling USA, 1750 E. Boulder St., Colorado Springs, CO 80909, tel.: 719/578-4581.

Dirt Rag, 460 Maple Ave., Springdale, PA 15144, tel.: 412/274-4529.

HPV News, International Human Powered Vehicle Association, P.O. Box 51255, Indianapolis, IN 46251.

Mountain & City Biking, 7950 Deering Ave., Canoga Park, CA 91304, tel.: 818/887-0550.

Mountain Bike Action, Hi-Torque Publications, 10600 Sepulveda Blvd., Mission Hills, CA 91345, tel.: 818/365-4512.

Police on Bikes News, P.O. Box 1038, Bel Aire, MD 21014-7038.

Pro Bike News, The Bicycle Federation of America, 1818 R St. NW, Washington, D.C. 20009.

Triathlete Magazine, 1415 3rd St., #303, Santa Monica, CA 90401.

Triathlon, Box 1587, Ann Arbor, MI 48106, tel.: 313/662-1000.

VeloNews, 1830 N. 55th St., Boulder, CO 80301, tel.: 303/440-0601.

Winning Bicycling Illustrated, 744 Roble Rd., Ste. 190, Allentown, PA 18103-9100, tel.: 215/266-6893.

Yellow Jersey Group Publications, 490 2nd St., Ste. 304, San Francisco, CA 94107. Publishes *California Bicyclist and Texas Bicyclist*.

Food for Athletes

Try the following publications to give you more information on nutrition for athletes.

The Athlete's Kitchen, by Nancy Clark, M.S., R.D. (New England Sports Publications: Boston, MA). Considered "essential."

Cycle Food: A Guide to Satisfying Your Inner Tube, by Laura Hefferon (Ten Speed Press: Berkeley, CA). Fun, full of advice and amusing drawings.

Gorp, Glop, and Glue Stew: Favorite Foods from 165 Outdoor Experts, by Yvonne Prater and Ruth Mendenhall (The Mountaineers Books: Seattle, WA). More food fun.

The Trekking Chef, by Claudine Martin (Lyons & Burford: New York, NY).

Good Reads

The Bicycle: Vehicle for a Small Planet, by Marcia D. Lowe (Worldwatch Institute: Washington, D.C.). Fascinating paper, full of facts about bicycling all over the world.

Bicycles up Kilimanjaro, by Richard and Nicholas Crane (Oxford Illustrated Press: London, England). And you thought you had gone everywhere.

The Bicyclist's Sourcebook, by Michael Leccese and Arlene Plevin (Woodbine House: Rockville, MD). Sort of a whole-earth catalog for cyclists.

Cyclist's Log (Bikealite, Silver Lake, NH). Information on touring and stretching and lots of space for you to write your own bicycling novel.

How to Shit in the Woods: An Environmentally Sound Approach to a Lost Art (Ten Speed Press: Berkeley, CA). We all want to leave our mark on the world. This is not the way to do it, however. For cyclists who camp or merely dash for a stand of pines, here's some practical advice. Superb cover.

In High Gear, The World of Professional Bicycle Racing, by Samuel Abt (Bicycle Books: San Francisco, CA). Fascinating, thorough account of racing.

Miles From Nowhere: A Round-the-World Bicycle Adventure, by Barbara Savage (The Mountaineers Books: Seattle, WA). Not to be missed.

Richard's Cycling for Fitness, by John Schubert (Ballantine Books: New York, NY). Comprehensive, friendly book by well-known expert.

Touring on Two Wheels, by Dennis Coello (Nick Lyons

Books: New York, NY). All sorts of touring information.

Tour of the Forest Bike Race, by H.E. Thomson (Bicycle Books: San Francisco, CA). Cartoons and whimsy make this book a not-for-kids-only explanation of bicycle racing.

Travels With Rosinante, by Bernard Magnouloux (Oxford Illustrated Press: London, England). An account of five years spent cycling round the world. Wonderfully written.

History

Around the World on a Bicycle, by Thomas Stevens (Seven Palms Press: Tucson, AZ). Abridged version of Steven's around-the-world trip in the 1880s.

Hearts of Lions: The Story of American Bicycle Racing, by Peter Nye (W.W. Norton: New York, NY). The definitive book on this subject.

How I Learned to Ride the Bicycle, by Frances E. Willard (Fair Oaks: Sunnyvale, CA). Fun book by a woman in her fifties who learned to bicycle in the 1800s.

King of the Road, by Andrew Ritchie (Wildwood, London). Excellent, respected history.

Major Taylor: The Extraordinary Career of a Champion Bicycle Racer, by Andrew Ritchie (Bicycle Books, Inc.: Mill Valley, CA).

On Your Bicycle, by James McGurn (Facts on File: New York, NY). Intelligent, sensitive history. Great book.

Mountain Bike Books

Get Ready to Go Mountain Biking, by Bikecentennial (Missoula, MT).

Mountain Bike Rides of the West, by Dennis Coello (Northland Publishing: Flagstaff, AZ).

Richard's Mountain Bike Book, by Charles Kelly (Ballantine Books: New York, NY).

The Mountain Bike Way of Knowledge, by William Nealy (Menasha Ridge Press: Birmingham, AL).

BIA's Mountain Bike Action Kit, by Bicycle Institute of America (Washington, D.C.).

Repair

Anybody's Bike Book, by Tom Cuthbertson (Ten Speed Press: Berkeley, CA).

The Bike Bag Book, by Tom Cuthbertson (Ten Speed Press: Berkeley, CA).

The Bike Repair Book, by Rob Van der Plas (Bicycle Books Inc.: Mill Valley, CA).

The Mountain Bike Repair Manual, by Dennis Coello (Lyons & Burford: New York, NY).

Richard's New Bicycle Book, by Richard Ballantine (Ballantine Books: New York, NY).

The Roadside Guide to Bike Repair, by Dennis Coello (Warner Books: New York, NY).

Safe Materials: Advocacy and Education

The Basics of Bicycling, by Linda Tracy and John Williams (Bicycle Federation of America: Washington, D.C.). Program for upper elementary school kids, which includes manual and video.

Captain Cycle and the Bike Ranger's Coloring Book (Outdoor Empire Publishing, Inc.: Seattle, WA).

Street Smarts: Bicycling's Traffic Survival Guide, by John S. Allen, Rodale Press, 33 E. Minor St., Emmaus, PA 18098, tel.: 215/967-5171. Great booklet. Available for $1 (attn. Michelle Gisolfi).

Effective Cycling, by John Forester (MIT Press: Cambridge, MA).

"How to Organize a Bike Day" (U.S. Environmental Protection Agency: Washington, D.C.). Free brochure with SASE from 410 M St. SW, Washington, D.C. 20460.

"Ten Little Bike Riders" (Outdoor Empire Publishing: Seattle, WA). Brochure.

National SAFE KIDS Campaign, 111 Michigan Ave. NW, Washington, D.C. 20010. □

23 GREAT BICYCLE TOURS

By Joe Kita, Senior Managing Editor of Bicycling *magazine.*

As the editor of *Bicycling* magazine, I am submersed in the world of cycling for at least 16 hours a day. My cycling subconscious continues to spin like a well-greased freewheel even as I sleep. So you would think that come vacation time I would want to get away from it all. Instead, I submerse myself further: I usually go on a bicycle tour.

The 23 tours that follow are personal favorites of mine. Most of them I've done. The others I've dreamed about doing. I've included rides for every ability level in just about every region of the country and the world. There are off-road tours and ones that never leave the pavement. There are one-afternoon rides and rides that could be summer-long affairs.

If I've done my job, there will be at least one ride that captures your imagination—a ride that plants a seed that grows into a tree that eventually becomes strong enough for you to climb and escape. If you've already been on a bicycle tour, you know what I'm talking about. If not, I invite you to learn.

New England Coast

Just 25 miles north of Boston begins a weekend tour that will take you along the coast of three states in one day. It starts in Beverly, Massachusetts, crosses the easternmost tip of New Hampshire, and ends in Kittery, Maine. In addition to ocean views, historic lighthouses, and country inns, there's the promise of genuine New England clam chowder and inexpensive lobster at trip's end.

From Beverly, follow Route 1A north through the towns

of Old Newburyport, Hampton, and Rye Beach. In Portsmouth, turn right onto Route 1B, then right again on Route 1 to cross the bridge to Kittery. In all, the trip covers 53 miles of paved roads and bike trails, much of it with the Atlantic Ocean brushing up against your shoulder. Spend the evening in Kittery, browsing through its many discount outlets, and ride back the next day.

Resources

Information: Bicycling Coordinator, Department of Transportation, State Office Building, Station 16, Augusta, ME 04333, tel.: 207/289-2954.

Tour organizer: Bikecentennial (Box 8308, Missoula, MT 59807) publishes a bicydist's map of the area for $2.95.

Reading: Fodor's Bed & Breakfasts and Country Inns and Other Weekend Pleasures: New England.

The Northeast Kingdom, Vermont

The Northeast Kingdom is the last truly rural corner of Vermont, a place of few towns and even fewer roads, where steep-faced mountains and fjord-like lakes (for example, Lake Willoughby) make it seem as if glaciers have only recently receded. It's also a place to which a good many flower children of the '60s escaped when the back-to-nature spirit of that time got washed away in the late '70s. They had good reason to believe that no one would look for them here.

Others are now discovering the Northeast Kingdom, lured by the sort of rural simplicity that has become increasingly gentrified in southern Vermont. Small villages, small lakes and ponds, back roads, the occasional country inn— it's all here. Get a good map and/or a good guide, and bring a bike you don't mind banging around on dirt roads. This is country to explore, to poke around in. If you stick to the main roads (in this case, Routes 16, 5A, and 105), one of the best stretches is the 50-mile ride from Barton, past Lake Willoughby, and on to Bloomfield on the New Hampshire border. The terrain is moderately up-and-down—no long mountain rides, but few long flat spots, either.

Resources

Information: Newport Chamber of Commerce, Newport, VT 05855, tel.: 802/334-7782.

Tour organizer: Vermont Bicycle Touring, Box 711, Bristol, VT 05443, tel.: 802/453-4811.

Reading: Fodor's Bed & Breakfasts and Country Inns and Other Weekend Pleasures: New England.

Lancaster County, Pennsylvania

If you avoid the main thoroughfares and stick to back roads, cycling through this part of southeastern Pennsylvania is like taking a trip back in time. Lancaster County is home to the world's oldest community of Amish, who along with their Mennonite cousins, are known as the Plain People or Pennsylvania Dutch. Their simple, austere life, popularized in the movie *Witness*, still involves working fields by hand and traveling by horse-drawn buggy. Although a tacky tourist culture has sprouted around the Pennsylvania Dutch, the back roads east of Lancaster and the towns of Intercourse, Blue Ball, Bird-in-Hand, Strasburg, and Paradise are still quaint and well-suited for riding, especially in the spring and fall when farming activity peaks.

You'll pedal through covered bridges, pass one-room schoolhouses, and have the opportunity to refuel with homemade root beer and shoo-fly (molasses and crumb) pie at roadside stands. But perhaps most satisfying is the perspective you'll gain on modern society and what has been lost with progress.

Resources

Information: Pennsylvania Dutch Visitors Bureau, 501 Greenfield Rd., Lancaster, PA 17601, tel.: 717/299-8901 or 800/735-2629.

Tour organizer: Lancaster Bicycle Touring, Inc., 3 Colt Ridge La., Strasburg, PA 17579, tel.: 717/396-0456.

Reading: "Pennsylvania Bicycling Guide," available from the Department of Transportation, Sales Store, Box 2028, Harrisburg, PA 17105.

Chesapeake & Ohio Towpath Trail, Washington DC, to Maryland

This 185-mile trail winds from the Georgetown section of Washington, DC, to Cumberland, Maryland, following the C&O Canal and the Potomac River. Not only will it amaze you that such a picturesque escape can be found so close to the congested national capital, but you'll be pedaling through a region infused with Civil War history. This trip is a lesson in the Civil War from the saddle of a bike.

For instance, sites along the route include Harper's Ferry, West Virginia, where John Brown tried to commandeer the federal arsenal in 1859. The Antietam Battlefield was the site of the war's bloodiest battle in 1863. Stonewall Jackson once tried to destroy the entire canal, in an attempt to sever a vital Northern artery.

Today, the canal, with its 74 locks, is a National Historic Park. There are well-maintained campsites about every 5 miles and many convenient access points. The towpath is mostly hardpack, but spring rains can turn some sections to mud, so mountain or hybrid bikes are recommended. This is a good trip for bikepacking novices and veterans alike.

Resources

Information: C&O Canal National Historical Park, Box 4, Sharpsburg, MD 21782, tel.: 301/739-4200.

Natchez Trace Parkway, Tennessee to Mississippi

Imagine 450 miles of smooth blacktop where commercial vehicles and billboards are banned, car traffic is minimal, and a 50-mph speed limit is strictly enforced. Sounds like a dream, but it's in fact a reality—witness the Natchez Trace Parkway, which begins in Nashville, Tennessee, and ends in Natchez, Mississippi. It's been called the South's premier cycling route, winding through valleys of rustic bliss and peace. There's a historical tinge to the Trace as well, as the road approximates an old trail used first by Choctaw and Chickasaw Indians.

Because there aren't any restaurants, hotels, or stores along the Trace, there usually is relatively little traffic. But plan on some extra riding: You'll have to detour into adjoining towns for lodging and amenities. It can also get hot and humid in this part of the country during the summer, so spring and fall are the best riding times.

Resources

Information: Natchez Trace Parkway Visitor Center, Rte. 1, NT-143, Tupelo, MS 38801, tel.: 601/842-1572; a cycling map is available for $2.

Tour organizer: Classic Bicycle Tours, Box 668, Clarkson, NY 14430, tel.: 716/637-5970 or 800/777-8090.

Rail Trails, Wisconsin

Think of the vast railroad network that was instrumental in the growth of this country. Now consider how much of it's being used today. Over the past 60 years, half of the 300,000 miles of track that crisscross this nation has been abandoned. Of this unused 150,000 miles, one-third has already been sold and another third is so remote that it's useless.

This leaves 50,000 miles of abandoned rail routes waiting to be converted to bike trails. The Rails-to-Trails Conservancy is a nationwide, nonprofit organization dedicated to doing just that. And nowhere has it been more successful than in Wisconsin, where 555 miles of "rail trails" exist. The two most popular are the Glacial Drumlin State Park Trail, which spans 47 miles from Madison to Milwaukee, and the Elroy Sparta State Park Trail, which covers 32 miles between the rail towns from where it draws its name. Both have a crushed limestone surface suitable for any type of bike, no vehicular traffic, and stunning rural scenery. For instance, the former passes through or near four wildlife areas and two state forests, while the latter features three giant tunnels and 34 trestles and bridges. In all, there were 3,300 miles of rail trails in 36 states as of July 1991. Chances are good there's a section near you.

Resources
Information: Rails-to-Trails Consevancy, 1400 16th St. NW, Suite 300, Washington, DC 20036, tel.: 202/797-5400.

Tour organizer: Timberline Bicycle Tours, 7975 E. Harvard #J, Denver, CO 80231, tel.: 303/759-3804.

Reading: A Guide to America's Rail-Trails, *published by Rails-to-Trails Conservancy.*

Durango, Colorado

In the 1800s, the lure of gold and silver brought hordes of prospectors to the San Juan Mountains in the southwest corner of Colorado. Durango was their base camp—a classic, Old West town fueled by whiskey and the promise of wealth. Today, mountain bikers are descending on Durango as eagerly as prospectors once did. They come to explore a maze of old mining trails the treasure-seekers left behind in the mountains. And they say what can be found—single-track intimacy, pure solitude, and the beauty of a mountain world rising well above 10,000 feet—is every bit as precious as the gold nuggets of yore.

Resources

Information: Durango Area Chamber of Commerce, 111 S. Camino del Rio, Durango, CO 81301, tel.: 303/247-0312.

Tour organizer: San Juan Hut System, Box 1663, Telluride, CO 81435, tel.: 303/728-6935.

Moab, Utah

Moab is the southwestern Mecca of mountain biking, and thousands of off-road cyclists make a trip here an annual pilgrimage. What they come to ride is a challenging 12-mile stretch of sandstone known as the Slickrock Trail. Originally used by motorcyclists, the course is marked by painted dots to keep riders on course and away from cliff edges.

Why travel deep into the Southwest for such a brief encounter? Well, depending on your riding skill, those few miles can take anywhere from two to five hours to complete. That's because the smooth, rounded rock and sharp drop-offs demand expert balance and bike handling, and you must semideflate your tires to maintain traction.

In addition, this triangle of land between the Green and Colorado rivers has a lot more to offer the off-road tourist. Canyonlands and Arches national parks are nearby, and their spectacular, canyon-rock settings and vast expanses of river-cut sandstone make for riding as challenging as the Slickrock Trail trip. If you want riding companionship, an annual Canyonlands Fat Tire Festival is held each October against the backdrop of freshly snow-capped mountains.

Resources
Information and tour organizer: Rim Tours, 94 W. First N, Moab, UT 84532, tel.: 801/259-5223.

Napa Valley, California

This verdant region northeast of San Francisco is one of the most popular bicycle touring destinations in the country. For good reason: Not only is it beautiful, but it's also home to a multitude of famous wineries such as Robert Mondavi and Christian Brothers. On a crisp summer morning, you can see the grapes glistening in the sunshine and smell their sweetness. Many wineries offer tastings and tours (some free), so save room in your panniers for the bottles you'll inevitably buy.

The valley is best suited to touring at an easy pace, and it's an ideal trip for the novice cyclist. Starting in Napa, you can spend a long weekend pedaling the flat, 25-odd miles to Calistoga, visiting the vineyards and staying in quaint country inns. The main thoroughfare (Route 29) can become very congested during the peak summer tourist season, so try to come in the early fall. For more challenging riding, the roads leading to and around Lake Berryessa to the northeast are scenic, forested rollers guaranteed to burn away the guilt and the calories from all that sipping.

Resources

Information: Napa Chamber of Commerce, 1556 First St., Napa, CA 94559, tel.: 707/226-7455.

Tour organizer: Backroads Bicycle Touring, 1516 5th St., Berkeley, CA 94710, tel.: 415/527-1555 or 800/245-3874 outside CA.

Monterey Peninsula, California

There's no reason why you should have to experience the famous "17-mile Drive" of California's Monterey Peninsula in a car. The privately owned area is great for cycling, although there are restrictions on where you can enter and a nominal fee. Once inside the gates, you follow a well-marked, smoothly paved road that winds past the crashing Pacific and some of the most famous golf courses in the world, including Pebble Beach and Spyglass. (Too bad a set of golf clubs can't be lashed under a top tube.) There are also magnificent cypress groves and mansion-like homes with storybook names such as "Paradise Found" and "Once Upon a Time."

171

The cycling is generally flat and easy, and because of strictly enforced speed limits, motorists are usually courteous to cyclists. You may want to pedal the drive in both directions, making for a 34-mile day, so as not to miss any of the scenery. In nearby Carmel (the town that elected Clint Eastwood mayor), there's lots of eclectic shopping, people-watching, and eating.

Resources
Information: Monterey Peninsula Chamber of Commerce, 380 Alvarado St., Monterey, CA 93940, tel.: 408/649-1770.
Reading: Fodor's California '92.

Pacific Coast Highway, California

This is a dream tour, ranking in the same exalted category as pedaling cross-country or cycling through France. It's a ride of passage for anyone with a set of panniers, a road atlas, and an adventurous spirit.

Famed Highway 1 (the official designation) snakes the length of the California coast. In the south, the beaches of Newport, Huntington, and Malibu showcase the laid-back West Coast lifestyle. Farther north, the Los Padres National Forest, Point Reyes National Seashore, and Humboldt Redwoods State Park display a rawer beauty. Along the way are points of interest such as William Randolph Hearst's San Simeon mansion, mountain biking's reputed birthplace in Marin County, the whale-watching headlands around Mendocino, and the frothing surf and squealing seals far below Bixby Bridge in Big Sur.

This tour takes muscle. Whether you're doing the entire highway (1,000 or so miles), as Greg LeMond did in preparation for the '91 racing season, or just a particularly scenic section such as Morro Bay to Monterey, you'll need a high level of fitness, a dependable bike, and a strong stomach for heights and high speed. At times, you'll be riding a tightrope of a white line separating the crashing Pacific from the humming traffic. A spring or fall trip will minimize the motorized stress, but the challenges are a small price for such grandeur. Go ahead. Quit your job and live.

Resources

Information: California Department of Transportation, Box 942874, Sacramento, CA 94274, tel.: 916/653-0036; ask for free map of northern section and bibliography.

Tour organizer: Backroads Bicycle Touring, 1516 5th St., Berkeley, CA 94710, tel.: 415/527-1555 or 800/245-3874 outside CA.

Reading: Fodor's California '92; Fodor's Bed & Breakfasts and Country Inns and Other Weekend Pleasures: The West; Hidden Coast of California *(Ulysses).*

Crater Lake, Oregon

Eight thousand feet above sea level, with the sky so close you may want to duck your head, is a 33-mile ride that will leave you (perhaps literally) breathless. Oregon's Crater Lake was formed when a giant volcano collapsed into itself millions of years ago and gradually filled with water. The water is the color of the darkest blues and is said to be almost 2,000 feet deep, with warm springs and mysterious marine life lurking in its depths.

The landscape surrounding this national park is dotted with other volcanoes, high desert, and, far below, rolling woodland. In all, it's one of those natural cathedrals where

173

you tend to speak in whispers.

The two-lane road that traces the lake rim is smooth and clean-shouldered. But traffic can get heavy during the peak tourist months (watch out for the sideview mirrors on those campers) and a brisk wind, some challenging hills, and the thin air will test your cycling fitness. It's an awesome experience that even photographs can't re-create adequately.

Resources

Information: Crater Lake National Park Headquarters, Box 7, Crater Lake, OR 97604, tel.: 503/594-2211.

Tour organizer: Timberline Bicycle Tours, 7975 E. Harvard #J, Denver, CO 80231, tel.: 303/759-3804.

Reading: Fodor's National Parks of the West.

Mt. Haleakala, Hawaii

The ride begins in the dark, 10,023 feet above the island of Maui, atop the world's largest dormant volcano—a legendary mountain that locals call "House of the Sun." As dawn pinkens the cloud tops, you strap on your helmet, zip up your windbreaker, and board a bike for the downhill cruise. After a few pedal strokes you begin a descent that lasts three hours, covers 39 miles, and has more hairpins than a Honolulu beauty salon. The chill of the morning air and the thrill of the descent are likely to turn your knuckles white.

Although speeds are limited for safety and the cost of the eight-hour excursion approaches $100 per person (including meals, equipment rental, and transportation to the summit, available through several day-trip organizers), it's an exhilarating experience, especially for novice cyclists. The views, the volcanic landscape, and the fauna within Mount Haleakala National Park are stunning, so the trip from sun to sea offers plenty of opportunities to pump some blood into those white knuckles by clicking a camera shutter. For those who prefer a stiffer challenge, there's a "Cycle to the Sun" bike race up the mountain each Labor Day.

Resources

Information: Haleakala National Park Headquarters, Haleakala Crater Rd., Box 369, Makawao, Maui, HI 96768, tel.: 808/572-7749.

Tour organizer: Cruiser Bob's, 99 Hana Hwy., Box B, Paia, Maui, HI 96779, tel.: 808/579-8444. For more extended tours in Hawaii: Bicycle Adventures, Dept. O, Box 7875, Olympia, WA 98507, tel.: 206/786-0989.

Atlantic Provinces, Canada

Nova Scotia, Newfoundland, and Prince Edward Island (PEI, for short) are three of the friendliest places on earth. The warmth of the townspeople is more than enough to compensate for the often brisk weather. Jutting into the Atlantic Ocean off the coast of New Brunswick, each has its share of rustic fishing villages, majestic lighthouses, rugged coastlines, and great whale- and bird-watching. There are also numerous crafts shops and art studios, plus a vacation's worth of lobster restaurants, where seafood is as fresh as the day's catch.

You can tour all three areas in a couple of weeks or spend an entire vacation cycling in just one. PEI, for instance, is a small, flat island with only 123,000 inhabitants. Each of its three counties has a circular scenic route of about 120 miles. A ferry ride takes you to Newfoundland, where the cycling can be just as relaxing if you avoid the Trans-Canada Highway between 9 and 5. Nova Scotia is much larger and more developed, but there's a multitude of lakes, game sanctuaries, and national parks in the interior. The best-known cycling route here is the rugged loop around Cape Breton Island. For an easier ride with more towns along the way, follow the southeast coast. For unique accommodations stay on a "tourist farm," where you'll become part of the family and play farmer, milking the cows.

Resources

Information: Canadian Cyding Association, 1600 James Naismith Dr., Suite 910, Gloucester, ON K1B 5N4, tel.: 613/748-5629.

Tour organizer: Vermont Bicyde Touring, Box 711, Bristol, VT 05443, tel.: 802/453-4811.

Reading: Bicycle Tours in Nova Scotia, *published by Bicyde Nova Scotia (Box 3010 Sout, Halifax, NS B3J 3G6, tel.: 902/425-5450);* Cycling the Islands, Prince Edward Island and the Magdalen Islands *(available through the Canadian Cyding Association).*

Rift Valley, Kenya

In most parts of the world, a bicycle tour is simply a bicycle tour, but when you're pedaling in the wilds of East Africa, it becomes a cycling safari. Northwest of Nairobi are two game reserves—Hell's Gate National Park and Lake Bogoria—where you're free to ride through the habitat of nonthreatening wildlife. You'll encounter giraffe, zebra, and gazelle at Hell's Gate and millions of flamingos at Bogoria. It's easy to imagine yourself stalking game in the footsteps of Teddy Roosevelt and Ernest Hemingway, albeit this time—excuse the pun—as a "big chain" hunter. There's also a strong cultural appeal to this trip; anthropologists call this part of the world "the cradle of mankind."

It's still not advisable to take to the roads alone, but about a half-dozen companies specialize in bicycle trips through the Rift Valley. On a bicycle there are no windows or engine roar—the stuff of motorized safaris—to obscure the hyena's laugh or the lion's roar. It's truly a wild ride.

Resources
Information and tour organizer: Bicycle Africa, 4887 Columbia Dr. S, Seattle, WA 98108, tel.: 206/628-9314.
Reading: Bicycling Africa *(available through Bicycle Africa).*

Katmandu Valley, Nepal

In the 1950s, climbers came to Nepal to make first ascents of the world's highest peaks. In the '60s, a new wave of new-age visitors came seeking spiritual enlightenment. The '70s and '80s ushered in the age of trekking.

So what's new in Nepal in the '90s? Mountain biking is catching on, which should come as no surprise in a high-mountain world interconnected by back roads and single-track trails. What's not new are the same elements that have drawn travelers to Nepal in the past: mountain scenery to take one's breath away, the Buddhist culture, and ancient temples, villages, and terraced fields clinging to steep hillsides.

The riding can be strenuous, though it need not be if you stick to the lower valleys as they reach from Katmandu to the Himalayan foothills. And you can combine bike touring with trekking at higher elevations. Just because it's the '90s doesn't mean trekking has become passé. Keep in mind, however, that the altitude, whether you're on a bike or on foot, can be tough. Allow several days to acclimatize to this thin-air world in order to appreciate fully the scenery and spirit of Nepal.

Resources

Information: Embassy of Nepal, 2131 Leroy Pl., Washington, DC 20008, tel.: 202/667-4550.

Tour organizer: Above the Clouds, Box 398, Worcester, MA 01602, tel.: 508/799-4499 or 800/233-4499 outside MA.

Readings: Fodor's The Himalayan Countries; A Guide to Trekking in Nepal *(Mountaineers).*

Dordogne River Valley, France

East of Bordeaux and a few hundred kilometers south of Paris is a region unsurpassed in its combination of scenery, history, and cuisine. The Dordogne region, deriving its name from the wide river that flows through it, is among the oldest inhabited areas on earth, with ancient cave dwellings to explore.

The road along the Dordogne River winds flat and smooth through the towns of Bergerac, Montignac, and Brive. The road along the nearby River Lot passes through the villages of Figeac and Cahors, covering similarly easy-riding terrain. These are among the most popular cycling routes in France, and you'll see many other two-wheel tourists, as well as villagers pedaling home from market with long, thin loaves of bread.

You can spend weeks cycling here at a leisurely pace, but if you want more challenge, leave the valleys and head up into the surrounding hills through a farmer's world of hay fields and stone houses. The wine is red and rich, and the food—pâté, truffles, pastries—is as good as anywhere in France.

Resources

Information: French Government Tourist Office, 610 Fifth Ave., New York, NY 10020, tel.: 900/990-0400.

Tour organizer: Classic Bicycle Tours, Box 668, Clarkson, NY 14430, tel.: 716/637-5970 or 800/777-8090.

Reading: Fodor's France '92; Biking through Europe, *by Dennis and Tina Jaffe (Charlotte, VT: Williamson Publishing Co., tel.: 802/425-2102 or 800/234-8791).*

Tour de France Route

For the Walter Mitty in all of us, here's a tour that will bring you closer to the world's greatest bicycle race than you ever dreamed possible. A typical July morning begins by riding all or part of the day's race route. This may include the famous time trial course around Lac de Vassiviere where Greg LeMond won the '90 Tour or one of the famous climbs such as L'Alpe d'Huez or the Tourmalet where even great riders have been humbled. Early-arriving fans will cheer as if you were part of the real peloton, and you'll experience first-hand what a demanding event the Tour really is. You can do all or just part of the 2,000-plus miles of the three-week Tour, and ride as much or as little as you want. Full sag support and qualified guides are provided.

Resources

Information and tour organizer: Breaking Away Tours, 1142 Manhattan Ave., Suite 253, Manhattan Beach, CA 90266, tel.: 213/545-5118.

Reading: Breakaway: On the Road with the Tour de France, *by Samuel Abt (New York, NY: Random House).*

Rhine River Valley, Germany

Gliding along the Rhine on the seat of a bicycle, it's easy to get intoxicated by the fragrance from vineyards sloping down to the river. Regions such as the Rheingau (north of Mainz) are renowned for producing some of Germany's finest wines, which undoubtedly you'll discover for yourself. A good time to come is in late September and October, a season of wine festivals along the Rhine and its sister river, the Moselle.

You can follow the Rhine for 120 miles along a succession of country road, bike paths, and highways from Cologne south to Mainz. Although the river roads are clotted with traffic during the summer, a bicycle path parallels Route B9 along the western bank for much of the way. Among the highlights are the many castles between Rüdesheim and St. Goar and the rocks upon which the famed Lorelei was said to have lured Rhine boatsmen to their death. For an unforgettable view of the river, pedal any side road or path leading up through the vineyards. And if you want to add a few miles to the trip, continue south to Heidelberg, its charming brick streets and church spires tucked between the mountains and the Neckar River.

Resources

Information: German National Tourist Office, 747 Third Ave., New York, NY 10017, tel.: 212/308-3300; Federation of German Cyclists (Bund Deutsche Radfahrer eV), Otto-Fleck-Schneiselt W-6000 Frankfurt 71, tel.: 011/49-69-678-9222.

Tour organizer: Euro-Bike Tours, Box 40, Dekalb, IL 60115, tel.: 815/758-8851.

Reading: Biking through Europe, *by Dennis and Tina Jaffe*

(Charlotte, VT: Williamson Publishing Co., tel.: 802/425-2102 or 800/234-8791).

Western Ireland

Try to envision Ireland in its most wildly romantic light: green fields demarcated by rambling stone walls, rugged mountains, lakes, the sea crashing against stone bluffs, old villages, old castles. It all comes together in just a couple of hundred miles of cycling in Ireland's southwest, where fingerlike peninsulas jut out into the Atlantic Ocean.

The Ring of Kerry is perhaps the best-known coastal route here, but because of its popularity, it can be jammed with traffic in the summer. To avoid crowds, head for the less commercial Dingle Peninsula, where Gaelic culture is alive and well. The 104-mile loop around the peninsula (starting in Killarney) is Ireland's true wild west: a place of grand scenery and charming guest houses.

The biggest question mark here is weather. It can be cloudy, damp, and cool even in summer, in accordance with the best traditions of Irish weather. The starkly beautiful seaside cliffs may simply seem doleful if poor weather sets in—that's the time to head to Muckrose House near Killarney, a folk museum set on a 40,000-acre estate—or disappear into a pub.

Resources

Information: Irish Tourist Board, 757 Third Ave., New York, NY 10017, tel.: 212/418-0800; Cyclists' Touring Club, Cotterel House, 69 Meadrow, Godalming, Surrey GU7 3HS, UK.

Tour organizer: Vermont Bicycle Touring, Box 711, Bristol, VT 05443, tel.: 802/453-4811.

Reading: Fodor's Ireland '92.

Northern Italy

The Italians regard cycling almost as a second religion. Italy is known for the great racers it's fathered, the beautifully built bike frames and components it has given the world, and the passion of its racing fans (the *tifosi*) as they cheer a pro in the peloton—or even you—up a steep climb.

Cycling in Italy is like playing softball in Yankee Stadium or touch football on a cold Sunday afternoon in Green Bay. You'll be passed by strings of colorful club riders humming along in a perfect pace line. You'll be toasted with glasses of grappa by old wrinkled men who, despite their appearance, appreciate what it's like to pedal 60 fast miles in a day.

Perhaps the most beautiful riding in the entire country can be found in the Dolomite Mountains and the regions of Venetia and Lombardy bordering Switzerland and Austria. It's rugged country, with sharp, stark peaks from which the multitude of lakes below can look like mere puddles. Narrow roads wind their way around it all, testing your fitness—and nerve—with switchbacked climbs and daring descents.

For rugged, Dolomite scenery, one of the best sections to ride is the 60-or-so miles from Bolzano to Cortina d'Ampezzo—so long as you make a point of sticking where possible to side roads and avoiding the heavily trafficked Dolomite Road. For a gentler ride, try the 60 miles south from Bolzano to Lago di Garda in Italy's Lake District.

Beware of unlighted tunnels, unannounced by signs, that cut through the mountains. And wave to the *tifosi*.

Resources
Information: Italian Government Travel Office, 630 Fifth Ave., Suite 1565, New York, NY 10011, tel.: 212/245-4822.

Tour organizer: All-Adventure Travel, Box 4307, Boulder, CO 80306, tel.: 303/499-1981 or 800/537-4025.

The Netherlands

Holland is tabletop flat, no low gears required. Your mother could bicycle the Netherlands. In fact, invite your grandmother along. Because of the terrain and a well-developed system of bike paths, Netherlanders commute to work, do their shopping, take their babies to the doctor, even haul farm equipment by bike. About the only bad things you can say about cycling in Holland is that some bike paths could be better marked and that the wind seems forever in your face.

For a taste of Holland cycling, try the 130-mile loop from Amsterdam through Utrecht, Gouda, Rotterdam, The Hague, and back to Amsterdam. One of the best times of year to come is April and May, when the tulip fields are in bloom, most notable in the region south of Haarlem. A 190-mile loop north of Amsterdam takes you past the beach resorts, but winds off the North Sea can make this northern loop chilly in spring; it's better suited for a summer ride.

Resources

Information: Royal Dutch Touring Club, Postbus 93200, 2509, BA's-Gravenhage, The Netherlands; Bikecentennial, 14 Jan de Bakkerstraat, 3441 EE Woerden, tel.: 011/31-34-341-7147.

Tour organizer: Europeds, Box 996, Boulder, CO 80306, tel.: 800/321-9552.

Reading: "Cycling in Holland," published by the Netherlands Board of Tourism (355 Lexington Ave., New York, NY 10017, tel.: 212/370-7367).

The South Island, New Zealand

You've probably heard about the ratio of people to sheep in New Zealand being something like one to 60. This means, of course, that there are lots of sheep and not many people, and sheep, fortunately, can't drive. As a result, even the main roads of New Zealand's South Island are relatively uncongested. In fact, you might see nearly as many bikers as automobiles, especially in the summer months of January and February. The word about New Zealand is getting around in cycling circles.

The South Island compresses an astonishing geographical variety into its relatively modest size. In a few hundred miles of riding, you can go from the open plains around Christchurch to the mountain-and-lake country around Queenstown, explore the fjords and rain forests around Milford Sound, and catch glimpses of the glacier-laden Southern Alps as you ride along the west coast. Despite the South Island's many mountains, the riding is mostly gentle to moderate, with few lung-busting mountain passes to traverse. To do the trip justice, plan on at least two weeks of touring. Plan also on taking a fishing rod; the trout fishing here is as good as it gets. Finally, plan on returning home with plenty of photos of sheep against spectacular backdrops.

Resources

Information: Canterbury Cyclists Association, Box 2547, Christchurch, NZ.

Tour organizer: Mountain Travel/Sobek, 6420 Fairmount Ave., El Cerrito, CA 94530, tel.: 510/527-8100 or 800/227-2384.

Reading: Fodor's New Zealand.